Malachi
HOPE AT THE END OF AN AGE

Malachi

HOPE AT THE END OF AN AGE

Ron Phillips

FOREWORD BY DR. ELMER L. TOWNS

Pathway
PRESS

Book Editor: Wanda Griffith
Editorial Assistant: Tammy Hatfield
Copy Editor: Cresta Shawver

Library of Congress Catalog Card Number: 2002114014
ISBN: 0-87148-378-5
Copyright © 2002 by Pathway Press
Cleveland, Tennessee 37311
All Rights Reserved
Printed in the United States of America

Dedication

I affectionately dedicate this book to

Pauline Baker,

a great Christian lady and a superb
mother-in-law.

Contents

Foreword

This book is expository preaching at its best. While it is not a critical commentary that explains the original text, the sermons are an outstanding example of Bible interpretation. Anyone reading these sermons or using these messages as a Bible lesson will be on solid ground for Biblical interpretation. Dr. Phillips has taken the text of Malachi, interpreted it properly, and applied it to Christians of the 21st century.

While not every topic in the Book of Malachi is covered in these sermons, Dr. Phillips has captured the heart of the book and communicates Malachi's passion for God that motivated him to write.

The author asks some probing questions for Christians today:

- In a world that is insensitive to the message of God, where do you stand?

- Do you question the word of God?

- Do you complain and make excuses for unfaithfulness?

He points out how vital it is that we take "the burden of the word of the Lord" (Malachi 1:1) to hear, as did Malachi, and stand as God's witness against unfaithfulness, disobedience and ungodliness.

When Dr. Phillips compares the problem of divorce in Malachi's day to the problem of divorce in our day, he brings the best of preaching to the pulpit. His discussion on the issue of divorce and remarriage is classic. Anyone who has problems with divorce should read these chapters carefully. Notice how the author does not lash out at divorce, yet he says: "God hates divorce, but God does not hate the divorcé!" Dr. Phillips upholds the sanctity of marriage, while giving hope to every divorcé—they can go and live in the will of God.

The subtitle, *Hope at the End of an Age*, correctly captures the meaning of this book. Remember, Malachi is the last book of the Old Testament, and the last verse ends with these words: "Lest I come and strike the earth with a curse" (4:6). However, this book does not end with a curse—it ends with hope. Phillips says those who are expecting the return of Jesus are living in the "Elijah generation"—the time when God will send Elijah to prepare for the coming of His Son. The "blessed hope" is coming soon (see Titus 2:13). We should lift up our heads and look to the clouds, for soon the Son of Man will appear. So the Book of Malachi points us to the coming of Jesus, which is the greatest hope ever.

May God bless those who read this book and teach its principles. May its message bring enlightenment to those who are spiritually blind, hope to those who are discouraged, and life to those who do not know Jesus Christ.

—Elmer L. Towns, Dean
School of Religion
Liberty University
Lynchburg, Virginia

General Outline of Malachi

I. A CALLOUS NATION (1:2-5)

Disregarded God's Love . . .

  A. Unrecognized Love (1:2)

  B. Unappreciated Love (1:3-5)

II. A CORRUPT NATION (1:6 – 3:15)

  A. A Corrupt Priesthood (1:6 – 2:9)

Dishonored God in . . .

    1. Attitudes of Defiance (1:6)

    2. Actions of Defilement (1:7-14)

    3. Administration of Duties (2:1-9)

  B. A Corrupt People (2:10 – 3:15)

Disgraced themselves in . . .

    1. Religious Idolatry (2:10, 11)

    2. Relationships That Destroy (2:12-16)

    3. Regard to Coming Judgment (2:17 – 3:6)

    4. Refusing to Obey God's Law (3:7-15)

III. A CONTRITE NATION (3:16—4:6)

Discovered God's mercy by . . .

A. Honoring the Name of God (3:16)

B. Having Their Name Written in the Book of Life (3:17—4:3)

C. Holding the Law of God in Their Hearts (4:4-6)

Acknowledgments

Anyone who preaches or teaches with any regularity must drink from many wells. Now past 50, I must confess that I cannot possibly remember all I have read and heard. I have probably forgotten some people who gave me wisdom and knowledge. Some unforgettable personalities include Dr. Sigurd Bryan, who taught me to love the Bible at Samford University; Dr. John Olen Strange, Dr. Thomas Delaughter and Dr. Harrison, who were my teachers of the Old Testament at New Orleans Seminary.

Separately and distinctly, I must thank the inimitable Dr. J. Hardee Kennedy, who made the Old Testament live! Though some of these men are in heaven, their words live on in my life.

I am also thankful to the late Abraham Herschel for his masterwork *The Prophets* and John Paterson for the *Goodly Fellowship of the Prophets*.

I owe a debt of gratitude to my able writing assistant, Margy Barber, who takes good things and makes them excellent.

Introduction

So, why blow the dust off an ancient book like Malachi and undertake a serious study of its words? What can an old prophet possibly say to a modern church at the beginning of a new millenium?

My prayer is that you will quickly see that the book penned by this prophet is vitally relevant to us in our current millenium. Through Malachi's message, we can learn how God speaks and acts at the end of an age. Malachi is a bridge between seasons in God's dealings with His people. It signaled a sunset on the old covenant, as God said His last word and made His final appeal to the hearts of His people, not to be heard again for 400 years. The next word out of God's mouth to His people and to the whole world would be the living, walking, breathing Son of God—Jesus!

God, who at various times and in various ways spoke in time past to the fathers by the prophets, has in these last days spoken to us by His Son, whom He has appointed heir of all things, through whom also He made the worlds (Hebrews 1:1, 2).

Malachi reminds us of the stark contrast between

the Old Testament curse and the New Testament message of grace. He conveys glimpses of both the righteous demands of a holy God and the capacity of God to show mercy and grace.

As we near the closing of this age of the church, we notice great similarities between our day and that of Malachi:

- A greater distinction between the faithful and the unfaithful

- Evidences of corrupted ministries

- A rise in divorce and break-up of the family unit

- A heightened awareness among the faithful of the imminent return of the Messiah

- A heightened focus on the issues of heaven and hell

- A greater need for the commitment of giving to God's work

All of these truths are found in Malachi. May God richly use this study to help you live in these last days.

The greatest demon is the "Principality of Persia". IRAN

A NATION AT SUNSET

It is vital that we take "the burden of the word of the Lord" to heart as did Malachi, and stand as God's witness against unfaithfulness, disobedience and ungodliness.

parallel - CYRUS
prophetic 1976
SHAH of IRAN - Jimmy CARTER

- SUNDAY - JAN 24, 2010 -

The burden of the word of the Lord to Israel by Malachi (Malachi 1:1).

" The Muslim MAFIA "
" Jimmy Carter Beck - Evans "

Sometimes its Not easy !!
" Embrace It !! "
TAKE up Your Cross . . . Quit Whining about it !!
No Fear, No Worry, Die to it !!

With this last book of the Old Testament, the sun was setting on a weary and corrupt nation. Through the centuries, Yahweh had clearly spoken, but this age of communication was drawing to a close as He was about to draw a curtain of silence between Himself and His people.

God's final message to Israel before the coming of the Messiah was entrusted to one called Malachi. This name comes from the Hebrew word *malac*, which means "to dispatch or send." The words *deputy* and *courier* also come from this Hebrew word, and it is also translated *angel* in the Old Testament.

Malachi was dispatched about 430 B.C. with a message that was God's last inspired word for 400 years. As a part of His judgment upon a people who refused to hear and to heed, God became silent and put His people in waiting. Three hundred years earlier, the prophet Amos spoke of such a judgment: " 'Behold, the days are coming,' says the Lord God, 'that I will send a famine on the land, not a famine of bread, nor a thirst for water, but of hearing the words of the Lord' " (8:11).

The day of Malachi was a time of great sadness. Judah had returned from Babylonian captivity, but the former glory of the nation had not been restored. Although the Temple had been rebuilt, the blessing that departed in Ezekiel's day had not returned. The joy and expectation that they had received at their return from captivity had turned to skepticism, faith turned to apathy, and national fervor and enthusiasm turned to indifference. The Book of Malachi reveals Israel's skeptical attitudes toward the love of God, the decrees of God, the worship of God and the service for God.

From Malachi's message, we learn the characteristics of a nation who is past her zenith and moving toward judgment. However, we not only see the dark clouds of judgment hovering over the nation, but we also see shining through those clouds the rays of hope in the God who is coming to redeem His people.

The Book of Malachi brings to light some striking

similarities between that age, when they were looking for the Messiah, and our own age, when we are
looking for His second coming! In the first verse of
the book, we learn the nature of the message needed by a people in their time of sunset.

A Difficult Message

"The burden of the word of the Lord . . ."

Malachi chose to use the word *burden* for the message being given. The Hebrew word is *massa*, used
66 times in the Old Testament. *Massa* is derived
from the word *nasa*, which means "to lift up and
bear a burden." While this word can be translated
oracle, the King James Version correctly translates it
burden.

Furthermore, the word means "a burden imposed
by a master." It is used to speak of donkeys and
mules carrying heavy loads for their owners. We
understand that Malachi was given a heavy message to carry to the people. The prophet was heavy-
laden like a beast of burden. The Lord, in giving
him this message, placed a great responsibility
upon him.

When used in reference to a prophet's message,
the word *burden* carries with it the idea of compulsion,
urgency and dread. The message the Lord gave

Malachi to deliver weighed so heavily upon him that he had to get it off his heart. With this message pressing upon him, Malachi had no choice but to lift up his voice and give the people the word.

In the use of the word *burden,* Malachi reveals the kind of sense of responsibility and urgency every preacher must have. The true prophet-preacher has an inner compulsion to deliver God's message lovingly and honestly. The voice of a prophet can be disturbing. It is difficult for God's preacher to discharge his burden upon the people he loves. However, if the preacher is to deliver the message of comfort and encouragement effectively, he must also give the message that discomforts and discourages when it is needed. If he would be the physician who heals, he must also be the surgeon who wounds in order that he may heal.

A Divine Message ✓

" . . . the word of the Lord . . ."

The burden Malachi delivered was the *word* of the Lord himself. It was not the word of Malachi, but the living message of Yahweh. The voice and pen of the prophet was aflame with the holy fire of divine inspiration.

The people had rebuilt the Temple, but their

relationship with God was still in ruins. It was Holy God speaking to His people about their spiritual shambles. This word is from Yahweh, for Malachi uses the covenant name of God. We recall from the Book of Exodus that God entered into covenant with His people. Scripture points out that the people had despised the covenant name *Yahweh* (Malachi 1:6). Therefore, the Lord said, "My name shall be great among the Gentiles" (v. 11). In Malachi's day, the rejection of the Messiah was already in evidence.

The walls of Jerusalem had been repaired and rebuilt, but Israel's covenant with Yahweh lay shattered upon the rocks of their unfaithfulness. In 2:8, we see that the priests had "corrupted the covenant of Levi." Scripture goes on to say that the people "profan[ed] the covenant" (v. 10). Furthermore, according to verse 14, they had broken the marriage covenant made before God. Thus, the Lord reminded His people that the covenant was sacred, and warned them that violation of it had put the nation in great jeopardy.

Through the course of time, the eternal God has not changed. The faithfulness He demanded of His people under the old covenant is still demanded from those of us who live today in the new covenant—those who are sealed by the precious blood of Jesus Christ. We are responsible to live in faithfulness to that covenant relationship. To dishonor it is to invite personal and national disaster.

A Declared Message✓

". . . to Israel by Malachi . . ."

Malachi declared the word from the Lord. The word translated *by* is the Hebrew word *yad*, which means "hand." This word speaks of authority. The hand was used to symbolize and express the receiving and discharging of authority. When one took an oath, it was done with an uplifted hand. When one prayed, it was often with an uplifted hand. The Lord entrusted His message into the hand of man. Malachi not only received the Lord's message, but he also received the authority to declare that message. He stood in God's authority and declared "the word of the Lord to Israel" (1:1).

Malachi preached to a nation whose sins were very much like those of our day. Though beloved of God, the people would not respond to God's love (1:2). Though they were God's children, they would not honor God (v. 6), and they were servants who would not obey. The ministers refused to lead the people. Divorce and the breakdown of the family were common (2:14). Though they were stewards, they refused to tithe (3:8-10). They were God's people, but all they could do was complain against God (v. 14).

Malachi declared that "the day of the Lord" was drawing near (4:5), and called God's backsliding people to repentance. He declared that those who were right with God would receive glory in that "day," and those who were away from God would face a time of gloom.

The Book of Malachi sets forth the message of God to an insensitive people. It records how the people questioned God seven times and that they refused to admit their failure and to repent. The people had no king, and they had no faithful priest. They had only one prophet, who faithfully declared God's message. According to this message, to go their way of rebellion would bring doom for the nation; to repent and return to God would bring God's restoration.

People with spiritual perception can see a strong comparison of Malachi's day to our day. As his nation was coming to the time of sunset, our world is doing the same. In a world that is insensitive to the message of God, where do you stand as an individual? Do you question the word of God? Do you complain and make excuses for unfaithfulness? In our day, it is vital that we take "the burden of the word of the Lord" to heart as did Malachi, and stand as God's witness against unfaithfulness, disobedience and ungodliness.

We've got to speak forth this . . .
—DECLARED MESSAGE

THOUGHT QUESTIONS

1. Israel had been delivered from captivity and then watched their glorious Temple rebuilt in splendor; but when the former glory of their nation didn't return right away, their joy and faith soon soured into skepticism and apathy.

Have you ever experienced a plunge in your trust and fervor toward God during a dry season in your life? Did this period of waiting come on the heels of a great deliverance or victory? What were the results in your own faith?

2. What steps can you take to prevent indifference and defeat from overtaking you in times of waiting on God? What promises of God can you stand on?

3. Malachi felt the weight and responsibility of a burden from the Lord. He knew that as God's messenger, he had to deliver truth whether it was pleasant or not.

Think back to a time when God's Spirit impressed or compelled you to action—whether it was a word, a deed or a change in attitude. Did you hesitate at His prompting, or did you completely surrender to His will? Ask God to continue to make you moldable clay in His hands.

CHAPTER TWO

FORGOTTEN LOVE

We need witnesses for God who will demon-
strate and declare what they have experienced
of God's grace and power.

"*I* have loved you," says the Lord. "Yet you say, 'In what way have You loved us?' Was not Esau Jacob's brother?" says the Lord. "Yet Jacob I have loved; but Esau I have hated, and laid waste his mountains and his heritage for the jackals of the wilderness." Even though Edom has said, "We have been impoverished, but we will return and build the desolate places," thus says the Lord of hosts: "They may build, but I will throw down; they shall be called the Territory of Wickedness, and the people against whom the Lord will have indignation forever. Your eyes shall see, and you shall say, 'The Lord is magnified beyond the border of Israel' " (Malachi 1:2-5).

T here is nothing more heartbreaking than unre-
quited love. Malachi's message was a great burden.
The weight of that burden is seen in the first statement,
"I have loved you. . . ." The depth of feeling in this cry
of Yahweh is beyond the scope of our understanding.

The nation had no king. Her priests were corrupt.
She was hearing the voice of the last prophet she
would hear for 400 years. What was God's last word
through His prophet? He declared again His love, to
which they had failed to respond. In these verses, we
find three attributes of God's love they had forgotten.

The Graciousness of His Love (1:2)

The word for *love* in this verse is the Hebrew

word '*ahab*. It is the same word for "ardent love." It means "a strong attachment to the beloved." In this case, emphasis is placed on the unconditional love of God for an undeserving people.

Undeserved love. The people had reached such a depth of degradation that they lost their sense of right and wrong. They called sin "righteousness," through the way they lived. They profaned God's name, robbed Him of His tithes and offerings, dishonored their marriage vows, and offered unworthy sacrifices. And God still loved them.

God's love for His people was based on His grace, not on their human merit. Is this not still true today? Paul said, "But God demonstrates His own love toward us, in that while we were still sinners, Christ died for us" (Romans 5:8). I have talked with many people through the years who thought God did not love them because they did not deserve His love. If we had to be worthy of God's love, there never would have been a single act of God to save us and provide for us.

Unconditional love. Malachi begins his book by using the example of Jacob and Esau from Israel's early history. God's choice to bless Jacob over Esau is hidden in the counsels of eternity, for Jacob had nothing in his person to commend him to God. We do not find a more inconsistent believer in the Old Testament. He was even known as a supplanter who used treachery to get what he wanted, but God's choice was not revoked. The Lord said to Rebekah their mother, "Two nations are in your womb, two peoples shall be separated from your body; one people shall be stronger than the other, and the older shall serve the younger" (Genesis 25:23).

The twins Rebekah conceived, Jacob and Esau, represented the two nations spoken of by Malachi. The nation of the Edomites, which sprang from Esau, has today basically ceased to exist, but God's plan for Jacob and Israel has prevailed. The Lord loved Jacob despite the fact that he appeared to be a most unlikely choice to become a great patriarch. The time came when Jacob dared to wrestle with God's messenger; the Lord had to *cripple* him before He could *crown* him.

God's love for us today is undeserved and unconditional. That's what Paul meant when he said, "For by grace you have been saved through faith . . ." (Ephesians 2:8). John says, "In this is love, not that we loved God, but that He loved us and sent His Son to be the propitiation for our sins" (1 John 4:10). John also said, "We love Him because He first loved us" (v. 19). God's election of His people is a divine mystery.

The Goodness of God's Love (1:2-4)

Israel replies to God's statement by questioning His love, "In what way have You loved us?" There are three possible reasons why Israel questioned God's love:

Ignorance. It could have been true that they did not know God loved them. There are many people who question God's love for them during difficult times, but we need to understand that adversity is not a sign that God does not love us.

Some people need to discover the love of God. Years ago, Bill was a grumpy bus driver in our ministry in New Orleans. A little ragged girl often followed him around before and after services and always hovered over his shoulder in the closest seat on the Sunday school bus.

One day, she lingered behind after everyone else had departed for Sunday school classes. Bill noticed her and gruffly asked, "What do you want?"

"Mr. Bill, won't you love me just a little bit?" she asked.

Bill melted when he realized how much that child loved him, and how much she needed to be loved. Do you realize how much God loves you?

Ingratitude. Israel probably knew about God's goodness, but it appears they failed to be thankful. It is easy to take our blessings for granted. The Lord made it clear to them how favored their nation was in comparison to Esau and the Edomites. The Nabateans, builders of Petra, had just conquered Edom and laid it to waste. Israel was still living in God's favor, even though they had sinned. Yet they questioned God's love with ungrateful hearts.

Indifference. It is also possible that the nation simply did not care anymore, for love can grow cold. In his diary, Thomas Carlyle wrote of his neglected wife, who died suddenly, "Oh, that I had but five minutes to tell you all. . . ." Carlyle had been indifferent to his wife's love, and when he finally awakened to it, he discovered that he was too late to respond to it. How easy it is for us to grow indifferent to the love of our God and Savior, Jesus Christ.

The Greatness of God's Love (1:5)

In verse 5, God promises that His people will *see* His greatness. The Hebrew word for *see* is *ra'ah*, which means "to see with understanding." It is more than a glance or casual look. It includes the ability to perceive and to discern what one is seeing. God said that one day the nation would see His greatness.

I believe this is a reference to the coming of Christ. Did not many see His greatness and glory when Jesus came the first time? I am convinced that this scripture speaks also of the second coming of Christ. The Bible says, "Behold, He is coming with clouds, and every eye will see Him" (Revelation 1:7). And to Israel, the Lord says, "And I will pour on the house of David and on the inhabitants of Jerusalem the Spirit of grace and supplication; and they will look on Me whom they pierced" (Zechariah 12:10). Can you imagine the majesty, glory, splendor and greatness He will display when they see Him?

Those who saw Him at His first coming declared His greatness from the border of Israel. The word went out to the ends of the earth. At His second coming, the whole earth will confess His greatness. What is the responsibility for those of us who have seen Him with the eye of faith? We should not only see what He has done for us, but we are also obligated to tell it to others.

The prevailing sin of the people of Israel was the sin of complaining. Instead of declaring the greatness of God, they questioned His grace and goodness. There are far too many witnesses for the world, the flesh and the devil. We need witnesses for God who will demonstrate and declare what they have experienced of God's grace and power.

Every believer has experienced the love of God through the work of Christ on the cross. God's love has been given freely without condition. There is no room for anyone to spurn such love through ignorance, ingratitude and indifference. Indeed, such love points beyond question to the greatness of God.

THOUGHT QUESTIONS

1. The need to be loved is basic to humans. If you were to conduct a simple Internet search on the topic of "building true love," you would receive over a million Web site options! You may realize your own need, but have you ever considered God's desire to be loved? Read again God's desperate cry to His people in Malachi 1:2-5. Have you ever sensed the passion of God's love for you?

2. Is there anything we can do to deserve God's love? Do you have difficulty comprehending that His love is given freely to you, without strings attached?

3. Consider the three roadblocks given in this chapter that prevented Israel from seeing God's love clearly: ignorance, ingratitude and indifference. Have any of these roadblocks appeared in your heart? Spend time in prayer today and ask God to reveal to your understanding His unconditional love!

Chapter Three

TIRED OF CHURCH

Were the whole realm of nature mine,
That were a present far too small!
Love so amazing, so divine
Demands my soul, my life, my all.

"*A* son honors his father, and a servant his master. If then I am the Father, where is My honor? And if I am a Master, where is My reverence? Says the Lord of hosts to you priests who despise My name. Yet you say, 'In what way have we despised Your name?'

"You offer defiled food on My altar, but say, 'In what way have we defiled You?' By saying, 'The table of the Lord is contemptible.' And when you offer the blind as a sacrifice, is it not evil? And when you offer the lame and sick, is it not evil? Offer it then to your governor! Would he be pleased with you? Would he accept you favorably?" says the Lord of hosts.

"But now entreat God's favor, that He may be gracious to us. While this is being done by your hands, will He accept you favorably?" says the Lord of hosts.

"Who is there even among you who would shut the doors, so that you would not kindle fire on My altar in vain? I have no pleasure in you," says the Lord of hosts, "nor will I accept an offering from your hands. For from the rising of the sun, even to its going down, My name shall be great among the Gentiles; in every place incense shall be offered to My name, and a pure offering; for My name shall be great among the nations," says the Lord of hosts.

"But you profane it, in that you say, 'The table of the Lord is defiled; and its fruit, its food, is contemptible.' You also say, 'Oh, what a weariness!' And you sneer at it," says the Lord of hosts. "And you bring the stolen, the lame, and the sick; thus you bring an offering! Should I accept this from your hand?" says the Lord.

"But cursed be the deceiver who has in his flock a male, and takes a vow, but sacrifices to the Lord what is blemished — for I am a great King," says the Lord of hosts, "and My name is to be feared among the nations" (Malachi 1:6-14).

B ehind the message of Malachi you can hear a plaintive cry, much like a brokenhearted father whose child has walked away, or a lover whose beloved has not returned that love. Few things are more painful than to love somebody and for them not to love you in return.

This is the cry coming from the very heart of God as He hears His own precious children saying of their service to Him, "What weariness it is!" We read that they "snuffed at" or "sneered at" the service of the Lord. Today we would say: "They turned their noses up at the Lord's service."

While this passage is directed to unfaithful priests who had become ungodly and, consequently, had become weary in serving God, we must understand that in the new covenant in Christ, all believers are priests! Peter declares, "You are a chosen generation, a royal priesthood" (1 Peter 2:9). Revelation 1:6 states that we are made "priests unto God" (KJV). The priesthood of the believer is a cardinal doctrine of the Christian faith. Therefore, the warnings in this passage must be applied to believers today. The tragic attitudes seen in those priests of Malachi's day can be observed in our modern church.

God had declared a twofold relationship to His people. First, He discusses the father/son relationship. He was their Father; the Israelites were His sons. It was mandatory in Hebrew culture that children honor their parents. Even deeper was the regard a son should have for his father. It could be a capital crime in Israel for a son to dishonor his father. The heart cry of the Lord to His people was, "I am your Father. Where is My honor?" Israel's attitude of disrespect and indifference was an insult to God's loving provision as Father.

The second relationship God refers to is that of the master/servant relationship. A servant was under obligation to be submissive and obedient. The word *servant* in this verse carries the connotation of a *bondslave*, or one who had been purchased and who owed his life to his master. Would not a servant respect his master if his very life and sustenance depended on that master? The Lord searchingly asks, "Where is My fear?" He called to their attention the respect that was due Him from them.

As Christians, we have the same twofold relationship to God. He is our heavenly Father by virtue of our new birth, and we are made sons of God by faith in Christ. God is our Master by right of redemption. He purchased us from the slave market of sin with the price of the precious blood of the dear Lamb of God, His Son, who died for us. We are under obligation to love Him, honor Him and obey Him.

Your life and worship will reflect who your God is and what your current relationship with Him is. When certain symptoms arise and church seems tiring to you, it is time to do a spiritual checkup and take a close look at your heart. Watch for these six warning signs.

Not Living Up to Your Potential

God looked at His people in Malachi's day and basically said, "You are My children. A son honors his father. You are My servants. Where is My honor? You are My priests. I have given you access into My presence." Somehow when they came to worship, it had become less than an encounter with God.

Maybe it had degenerated into performance. Maybe it had become ordinary and regular. Maybe they had forgotten the depth of His awesome glory and presence. Something was terribly wrong in what was going on in their worship.

They came to worship and had forgotten who He is—their Master, their Father, their King, their Lover. When you don't know who He is, soon you won't know who you are, and your own motivation and confidence will suffer.

Offering Less Than Your Best

The people of Israel were offering blemished sacrifices to God. In Exodus 12:5 and Leviticus 22, they had been taught that every sacrificial animal was to be without any flaws. It was to be a male of the best flock. This was vitally important because of the promise portrayed, the promise of God to give His perfect Son as the unblemished sacrifice for our sin. Peter said, "You were not redeemed with corruptible things, like silver or gold . . . but with the precious blood of Christ, as of a lamb without blemish and without spot" (1 Peter 1:18, 19). The One who would die for sin, Jesus, would be totally sinless; therefore, the sacrifice that pictured God's gift of His Son had to be without blemish.

However, these people disgraced God's altar with unfit sacrifices. Instead of bringing the best, they brought the worst of their flock. They had the audacity to bring animals that were lame, sick and wounded. Under Jewish law, such animals were to be thrown to the dogs. Instead, they were bringing this "dog food" to God!

The Lord will not tolerate our offensive spiritual sacrifices that cost us nothing. Our attitude toward Him is revealed by what we offer. To offer Him that which is cheap and inferior tells Him that His name, and all it represents, means nothing to us.

A pastor friend accepted the pastorate of a certain church in Alabama. Upon his arrival, he found certain areas of the building to be extremely substandard and in disarray, especially the church library. He discovered that the people had brought in dozens, if not hundreds, of volumes of books they had discarded from their own library shelves and attics. Not only were the books old and terribly worn, many of them were unfit to be in a church library! He and a staff member had to spend hours sorting and hauling away the unacceptable books.

There is another incident I'll never forget as long as I live. While waiting to speak in a revival, I sat in the front row. As a girl got up to sing a solo, she first made a brief apology: "I can't give it everything today because I'm going to Nashville to make a recording. You'll just have to forgive me. I didn't have time to memorize the words." I wanted to stand and reply, "Well, just sit down and let's go on with the service! Nashville gets your best and you're giving God your leftover scraps?"

If He is a great king, our lover and our Father, I don't want to bring Him anything cheap, tawdry and unworthy. God is not pleased with us, nor honored, when we give Him everything we do not value highly. We are simply giving Him leftovers. Our God deserves the best! To offer Him less is to reveal that we think little of Him. Our prayer should echo the great hymn:

Were the whole realm of nature mine,
That were a present far too small!
Love so amazing, so divine
Demands my soul, my life, my all.

Unanswered Prayers

When the offering of our heart in worship doesn't come with excellence, heaven is sealed and our prayers are not answered. Malachi wrote, "Entreat God's favor" (1:9). Prayer is not you begging God for something. It is adjusting your life to what He

wants, and letting Him lift up your chin. He stands
waiting to be the lifter of our countenance.

When your children get hurt, your first instinct
as a parent is to lift up their face and kiss them and
hug them and tell them it is going to be all right.
They came into your presence expecting that intimacy and comfort, and they received it. God, our
Father, is saying to us, "If you get right with Me, if
you really want to be in My presence, if you are not
tired of Me, if you will come in and pray, won't I
accept you favorably? Won't I lift up your chin?"

Losing the Spirit of Worship

Malachi 1:10 says, "'Who is there even among
you who would shut the doors, so that you would
not kindle fire on My altar in vain? I have no pleasure in you,' says the Lord of hosts, 'nor will I accept
an offering from your hands.'" Somehow the people had lost the spirit of true worship.

Jehovah was looking for someone honest enough
to say, "This isn't working. Let's just shut the door,
turn off the lights and go home." They weren't willing to change as a nation. Neither were they willing
to admit their worship had become stale, so God
did it for them. After the close of Malachi, we have

no evidence that God spoke or made His presence known to Israel for 400 years!

I don't want that to happen to me. I don't want God to come to me and say, "What's wrong with you, My child? You've lost your fire and enthusiasm for being in My presence. I don't want a stilted worship performance—I want *you!*"

Missing Opportunities for Service

The people had become tired of serving the Lord. Why? Their service was without the acceptance and blessing of God because of their spiritual condition. Theirs was a religion of convenience rather than a commitment to God.

If we fail to come with a pure offering, if we don't honor and glorify His name, we may miss our opportunity to be a part of His world-shaking destiny! Peter tells us that we are "a holy priesthood, to offer up spiritual sacrifices acceptable to God" (1 Peter 2:5). Spiritual sacrifices involve service that is of the Spirit of God and in His power. When we attempt to render service unto God without bothering to make sure we are yielded and clean before Him, such service is futile. To continue on in a life of religious formality, void of God's blessing of power and fruit, not caring that we do not have His favor, and not caring if we serve Him well, reveals a serious and sinful attitude toward God.

Blinded to a Kingdom Vision

Church becomes weariness when you no longer remember you are involved in a Kingdom operation. In Malachi 1:13 we read, " 'You also say, "Oh, what a weariness!" And you sneer at it,' says the Lord of hosts." Then God goes on to say, " 'But . . . I am a great King,' says the Lord of hosts, 'and My name is to be feared among the nations' " (v. 14).

It is critical for us to maintain a close worship experience with the Father, so that our future remains clear and filled with purpose. Solomon wrote, "Where there is no vision, the people perish" (Proverbs 29:18, KJV). It is time to look outside our denominational walls, our traditions, our comfort zones, and see that there is a great big kingdom all around the world with people who may have different methods than we do, but who have the same passion for the lost and hurting. Staying safely tucked inside our brick buildings behind our stained glass windows will only ensure that we become weary and complacent within the routines of worship—and our joy will be lost.

A number of years ago, I drove by a certain

church facility, and the parking lot was covered with garage sale merchandise. A sign was displayed that read, "HELP OUR BUILDING FUND." I noticed that a number of late-model cars and trucks—the newest that money could buy—were in the parking lot. It seemed to be an ironic picture. I couldn't help but ask myself, *Is that sacrifice? Is that love for the God of glory? Is that respect for the God of greatness? Does it honor the Lord to sell used goods that are no longer of much value in order to finance His work, while our best is reserved for our own pleasure?*

What kind of attitude does this reveal toward God? Let us never forget that He is the great King who deserves more than the leftovers of our time, money and talent. He is worthy of our all. His person, name and glory must not be forgotten!

Do you know how to stay happy in church? Chase God. Always come looking for what He is doing. Never forget to be a God-seeker with all your heart.

THOUGHT QUESTIONS

1. What twofold relationship to God was discussed in this chapter? Does either of these relationships have special meaning to you?

2. It is time for a spiritual checkup! Has church and service to God become mundane to you? Prayerfully consider each of these danger signs and jot down your thoughts under the following symptoms you feel have appeared in your own life:

- Not Living Up to Your Potential

- Offering Less Than Your Best

- Losing the Spirit of Worship

- Missing Opportunities for Service

- Blind to a Kingdom Vision

3. In what ways can you approach worship as a child chasing the Father?

Chapter Four

When Your Hero Becomes a Zero

Every Christian should find somebody to be transparent with and accountable to, so that they can always walk before God in that holiness of life.

"*And now, O priests, this commandment is for you. If you will not hear, and if you will not take it to heart, to give glory to My name," says the Lord of hosts, "I will send a curse upon you, and I will curse your blessings. Yes, I have cursed them already, because you do not take it to heart.*

"Behold, I will rebuke your descendants and spread refuse on your faces, the refuse of your solemn feasts; and one will take you away with it. Then you shall know that I have sent this commandment to you, that My covenant with Levi may continue," says the Lord of hosts. "My covenant was with him, one of life and peace, and I gave them to him that he might fear Me; so he feared Me and was reverent before My name. The law of truth was in his mouth, and injustice was not found on his lips. He walked with Me in peace and equity, and turned many away from iniquity.

"For the lips of a priest should keep knowledge, and people should seek the law from his mouth; for he is the messenger of the Lord of hosts. But you have departed from the way; you have caused many to stumble at the law. You have corrupted the covenant of Levi," says the Lord of hosts. "Therefore I also have made you contemptible and base before all the people, because you have not kept My ways but have shown partiality in the law" (Malachi 2:1-9).

There was a pastor in a mainline Christian denomination who preached the Bible as God's Word. Leaving his denomination, he moved to California and started his own church. Known as a "faith healer," he allegedly demonstrated all the wonderful gifts of the Spirit. However, he was the same preacher responsible for the Guyana atrocity—the man who led over 900 adults to commit suicide, and then did the same himself. His name was Jim Jones.

A number of years ago in the state of Oregon, a guru from India named Rajneesh led a cult movement of more than 7,000 people. He stated that anyone who is a Christian is insane. He lived in extreme and lavish luxury, keeping his followers as virtual slaves.

Some time ago, a popular Southern Baptist evangelist became engaged in an adulterous affair, left his wife, and became a motivational speaker. He was, for a time, associated with the avowed atheist, Madalyn Murray O'Hair, and was the keynote speaker at her Athens convention.

Over the past decade, various scandals of prominent leaders have embarrassed the Christian community. Jim Bakker, who was among those who fell, has admitted his wrongdoing. He now concludes that he had taken his eyes off Jesus.

What is it that causes ministers to go bad? Why will people follow leaders who are not living right? Malachi demonstrates how bad *leadership* causes bad *"followship."* The priesthood in Israel had gone bad and influenced the corruption of the nation. Why did it happen, and what were the results of this terrible situation? We will answer these questions by examining these nine verses.

The Covenant of the Priesthood (2:4-7)

Please note the word *covenant* in verses 4 and 5. It comes from the Hebrew word *berith*, which means "to cut a covenant." In today's language, we might say, "enter a contract with." A covenant was a contract between God and man, sometimes accompanied by signs, sacrifices and solemn oaths that sealed the covenant. The covenant carried a promise of blessings if kept, and the threat of curses if broken.

God made a covenant with Levi and his descendants who were to be priests in Israel. In these verses, we find the marks of the ideal priest. God promised life and peace (v. 5) to those whose lives met these characteristics and fulfilled these responsibilities. According to the Scriptures, a true priest was one who . . .

- Feared God
- Walked with God
- Spoke truth
- Witnessed to others
- Studied and proclaimed God's word.

These were God's requirements and expectations of those whom He called to be spiritual leaders. The acceptance of such responsibility was a serious matter to the Lord, and to most of the priests throughout Israel's history. Along with the demands, God imparted the promise of strength to meet His demands.

The Corruption of the Priesthood (2:8, 9)

In verse 8, the prophet gets to the very heart of "the burden of the word of the Lord" (1:1). We

cannot help but be reminded of Nathan's con-
frontation to King David after his adulterous affair
with Bathsheba and the murder of her husband.
We find the same bold and candid manner in
Malachi's message as he comes right to the point.
God was accusing the priests as culprits in Israel.
Three main areas in which the priests "corrupted
the covenant of Levi" (v. 8) are pointed out.

1. *The priests departed from God's way* (v. 8). This
phrase indicates several areas of departure. First,
they departed spiritually. They had gone out of
God's way and no longer walked with God. They
had become selfish and insensitive to their sin. They
no longer gave homage to God; rather, they sought
the homage for themselves.

Second, they departed morally. The word *corrupt*
is broadly inclusive. These priests corrupted themselves morally, because they had low moral stan-
dards that led to corrupt moral activities.

How does a leader go bad? Just as these priests
did: personal behavior opens doors or gives
ground to satanic attack. When leaders neglect the
Word of God (the Scriptures), they will question or
lose their sense of the authority of God. Gradually,
they may become insensitive to the will of God —
that is, what God desires to accomplish through

their ministries. Departing from the way of God, they become much like wandering sheep, prey to the ravenous wolves of destruction. We have the responsibility to pray for those in leadership, that the fires of devotion and love for Christ may continue to burn in their souls.

2. *The priests destroyed the faith of others* (v. 8). The most tragic result of these priests departing from God's way was that they "caused many to stumble." What power there is in a lofty position and the influence it bears! Volumes could be written relating how the power of influence was misused, causing others to fall. Our lives are either attractive and winsome, or else we are a hindrance to others. Paul said, "For none of us lives to himself, and no one dies to himself" (Romans 14:7).

The priests of Malachi's day touched the lives of a nation and led them down the paths of corruption. Those who do this are doubly responsible to God for themselves and for the ruin they cause in the lives of others. Jesus had some hard things to say to the Pharisees of His day who led others into error. He called them "blind guides" (Matthew 23:16, 24). Concerning their converts, He further said, "And when he is made [a proselyte], ye make him twofold more the child of hell than yourselves" (v. 15, KJV). Jesus also told them that they would "receive greater damnation" (v. 14). Corruption in the lives of leaders always begets corruption in the lives of those who succumb to the power of their evil influence.

3. *The priests deviated for material gain* (v. 9). In departing from God's way, these priests made differences in judgment, showing partiality. Their inconsistency in their rendering of judgment was for personal gain. The use of dishonest means to enhance one's own financial position is always a sure sign of corruption before Holy God.

The Curse on a Bad Priesthood (2:1-3)

In violating the covenant God made with the priests, they brought God's curse upon themselves. The curse was manifest in three ways:

1. *The removal of God's blessings.* According to Scripture, whatever the priests chose to bless, God chose to curse. There was no God-given success to their priestly office. The corrupt leader always loses the favor and anointing of Almighty God.

2. *Their relations were affected.* We are reminded of God's word given in Exodus 20:5: "I, the Lord your God, am a jealous God, visiting the iniquity of the fathers upon the children of the third and fourth

generations of those who hate Me." Read the account of the wickedness of the sons of Eli and of the prophecy against the house of Eli (1 Samuel 2). Then think on these words from the Proverbs: "The curse of the Lord is on the house of the wicked, but He blesses the home of the just" (3:33).

3. *The revelation of their corruption was exposed* (v. 9). God exposed the corrupt priests in a public way. He had to reveal to the people that He did not condone the lives and activities of those who claimed to represent Him. In verse 3, God promised that they would literally *face* the pollution of the inferior and unfit sacrifices they accepted on God's behalf. The Lord said He would smear the dung of those animals upon their faces, and then take them out to the dung gate for public display and exposure before all the people. God will not allow that which is contemptible in His sight to go uncondemned. He says, "Be sure your sin will find you out" (Numbers 32:23).

What does this example say to us?

- Sin takes away the blessings of God.
- Sin affects our families.
- Sin will be exposed and judgment is inevitable.

In order to maintain the favor and blessings of God upon our lives and ministries, there are some things to which spiritual leaders should give serious attention:

1. *Hearers of the Word.* The psalmist David prayed, "Cause me to hear Your lovingkindness in the morning . . . cause me to know the way in which I should walk" (Psalm 143:8). The prayer in 119:133 should also be prevalent in our hearts today: "Order my steps in thy word" (KJV). Understanding, direction and wisdom to follow His Word can be gained by spending quality time in God's Word. This is not an option—we are obligated to do this.

2. *Heartfelt Commitment.* The first sign of spiritual deterioration could be a cold and insensitive heart toward the Lord, His Word and the people to whom we minister. I believe it is of utmost importance to put forth all the effort necessary to keep our hearts aflame with love, zeal and a sense of commitment to the task.

3. *Ministry That Glorifies God.* As priests unto God, let us keep our covenant with Him. The Great High Priest, the Lord Jesus, in the person of the Holy Spirit, lives in our hearts. May His ministry flow through us, and may we give no place to vanity and self-exaltation. Jesus prayed, "Father, glorify Your name" (John 12:28). Should not this be our example and attitude?

4. *Accountability.* Pastors and leaders too often

put themselves in such a lofty, restricted place that they have no one to confide in. This is a dangerous place to be. Every leader should become accountable to somebody.

My own executive pastor feels free to come to me with any concern he has about my personal or public conduct. He does it with a sweet and kind spirit, but in plain language. If something doesn't sound right or look right, Brother Jim will be certain to tell me. Whom are you accountable to? Who asks you the hard questions? Who could ask you, "How's your thought life?" and then follow through by praying with you about it and not telling anybody?

The reason so many people are ending up in a wreck is because on their way to the wreck, they couldn't tell anyone about their struggle for fear that they would be betrayed and destroyed. Every Christian should find somebody to be transparent with and accountable to, so that they can always walk before God in that holiness of life.

I want to finish well. Like Paul, I don't want to be a castaway. I don't want to come to that place where the Lord says, "I'm going to set you on a shelf. I can't use you anymore. Your attitude, your heart, your actions will not allow Me to use you."

If there is anything questionable going on in the

edges of your life, get rid of it now. I believe God is able to bring your life to fullness and usefulness, for He promised it in His Word: "He who has begun a good work in you will complete it until the day of Jesus Christ" (Philippians 1:6).

THOUGHT QUESTIONS

1. Unfortunately, most of us can name a respected leader—either well known or someone we know personally—who has fallen into sin. What causes leaders to go bad? Do we expect more from them than we do from ourselves?

2. What are the three curses upon the corrupt priests that Malachi listed? Do these consequences apply to each of us who sin?

3. A corrupt leader has the potential of guiding his or her followers into corruption also. In what practical ways should we use discernment and responsibility in placing ourselves under someone's authority? What specifically does God instruct us to pray for those who have leadership over us?

4. Do you have someone whom you can personally be accountable to, who can ask you the "tough questions" to encourage you toward a holier life?

CHAPTER FIVE

DIVORCE AND REMARRIAGE

PART 1

The divine ideal for marriage is clearly a life-long bond that unites husband and wife in a "one-flesh" relationship. The marriage union is a holy condition founded by God and is not to be dissolved at the will of man.

*H*ave we not all one Father? Has not one God created us? Why do we deal treacherously with one another by profaning the covenant of the fathers? Judah has dealt treacherously, and an abomination has been committed in Israel and in Jerusalem, for Judah has profaned the Lord's holy institution which He loves: he has married the daughter of a foreign god. May the Lord cut off from the tents of Jacob the man who does this, being awake and aware, yet who brings an offering to the Lord of hosts!

And this is the second thing you do: you cover the altar of the Lord with tears, with weeping and crying; so He does not regard the offering anymore, nor receive it with goodwill from your hands (Malachi 2:10-13).

Can a divorced person remarry? Should a divorcé serve in ministry? Should a woman leave her unfaithful, unbelieving husband?

A study seeking to answer these questions is always controversial and usually emotional. Divorce writes its misery across the lives of both the partners in the marriage and any children involved. The fruits of divorce include guilt, emptiness, loneliness and frustration. The injured parties end up struggling not only with these intense emotions, but also with the uncertainty of their future, both in new relationships and in their service in church ministry.

Rather than rehash tradition, we must look at what Scripture says. This study begins and ends with Scripture. Make no mistake about it: God hates divorce. But . . . *God does not hate the divorcé!* While Scripture stresses the permanence of marriage, let us also study what it says about life after a failure.

Old Testament

Unfortunately, the attitude of hatred seems to be the reigning attitude of many in the church toward those who have been through the pain of divorce. The divine ideal for marriage is clearly a lifelong bond that unites husband and wife in a "one-flesh" relationship. The marriage union is a holy condition founded by God and is not to be dissolved at the will of man.

Separations of this bond displease God and pose a serious threat to the social order. Read again Malachi 2:15, 16: "And let none deal treacherously with the wife of his youth. For the Lord God of Israel says that He hates divorce, for it covers one's garments with violence."

In Old Testament days, the law of Moses allowed a man to divorce his wife when she found "no favor in his eyes because he has found some uncleanness in her" (Deuteronomy 24:1). The primary purpose of this legislation was to prevent him from taking her again after she had married another man, which verse 4 says is "an abomination before the Lord."

This law was intended to discourage, rather than

encourage, divorce. A public document known as a certificate of divorce was granted the woman. This permitted her the right to remarry without civil or religious sanction. Divorce could not be done privately. Deuteronomy 24:1-4 says:

> When a man hath taken a wife, and married her, and it come to pass that she find no favour in his eyes, because he hath found some uncleanness in her: then let him write her a bill of divorcement, and give it in her hand, and send her out of his house. And when she is departed out of his house, she may go and be another man's wife. And if the latter husband hate her, and write her a bill of divorcement, and giveth it in her hand, and sendeth her out of his house; or if the latter husband die, which took her to be his wife; her former husband, which sent her away, may not take her again to be his wife, after that she is defiled; for that is an abomination before the Lord: and thou shalt not cause the land to sin, which the Lord thy God giveth thee for an inheritance (KJV).

The Mosaic Law called for severe penalties for certain types of "uncleanness." Adultery carried the death penalty by stoning for the woman. If a man believed that his wife was not a virgin when he married her, he could have her judged by the elders of the city. If they found her guilty, she could be put to death (see Deuteronomy 22:13-21).

Although a man was allowed to divorce his wife, the wife was not allowed to divorce her husband for any reason. Legally, the wife was bound to her husband as long as they both lived or until he divorced her (see 1 Corinthians 7:39).

New Testament

In Jesus' day, confusion prevailed about the grounds for divorce. Even the rabbis could not agree on what constituted the "uncleanness" spoken of in Deuteronomy 24:1. Followers of Rabbi Shammai believed adultery was the only grounds for divorce. Those who followed Rabbi Hillel accepted many reasons, including such things as poor cooking.

This was the sin Jesus was dealing with in much of His teaching on divorce. Pharisees were putting away their wives for reasons other than adultery. Furthermore, they were not giving the woman the required legal document called the "bill of divorcement." This document was the woman's permission to remarry and clear her reputation. This was an important document when you understand that a man divorcing a sexually unfaithful wife was not required to give her such a document. In fact, both adulteress and adulterer were subject to stoning, although this drastic measure was seldom carried out. Note the following incident in the life of Jesus:

> They said to Him, "Teacher, this woman was caught in adultery, in the very act. Now Moses, in the law, commanded us that such should be stoned. But what do You say?" This they said, testing Him, that they might have something of which to accuse Him. But Jesus stooped down and wrote on the ground with His finger, as though He did not hear. So when they continued asking Him, He raised Himself up and said to them, "He who is without sin among you, let him throw a stone at her first." And again He stooped down and wrote on the ground. Then those who heard it, being convicted by their conscience, went out one by one, beginning with the oldest even to the last. And Jesus was left alone, and the woman standing in the midst. When Jesus had raised Himself up and saw no one but the woman, He said to her, "Woman, where are those accusers of yours? Has no one condemned you?" She said, "No one, Lord." And Jesus said to her, "Neither do I condemn you; go and sin no more" (John 8:4-11).

Jesus defended this woman and forgave her. It is striking that the man who committed adultery with her was not present. Understand that Jesus' teaching in this area struck out at the male oppression in their relationships with women.

The key passage on the matter of divorce in the New Testament is found in the Sermon on the Mount:

Ye have heard that it was said by them of old time,
Thou shalt not commit adultery: But I say unto you,
That whosoever looketh on a woman to lust after
her hath committed adultery with her already in his
heart. And if thy right eye offend thee, pluck it out,
and cast it from thee: for it is profitable for thee that
one of thy members should perish, and not that thy
whole body should be cast into hell. And if thy right
hand offend thee, cut it off, and cast it from thee: for
it is profitable for thee that one of thy members
should perish, and not that thy whole body should
be cast into hell. It hath been said, Whosoever shall
put away his wife, let him give her a writing of
divorcement: But I say unto you, That whosoever
shall put away his wife, saving for the cause of for-
nication, causeth her to commit adultery: and
whosoever shall marry her that is divorced commit-
teth adultery (Matthew 5:27-32, KJV).

As you can see from the entire context, Jesus teaches that *lust* is declared to be adultery! In our day,
would a person who has lusted in his heart be per-
manently disqualified from service in the church?

Obviously, the man putting his wife away in verse
31 had already spotted another woman who struck
his fancy. Therefore, he dismissed an innocent wife,
compounding his sin by refusing to give her the bill
of divorcement, which would clear her reputation.
Thus, he actually was the adulterer, and what he

did was legally acceptable, yet the woman he put away would bear the stigma of adultery, as well as the man she married. Note the words "causeth her," which translate from the Greek word *poieo*, meaning "to make" — to produce, to construct, to form, to fashion, to be the authors of, or the cause.

As you can see, the woman who was put away was stigmatized through no fault of her own, as was her new mate. Jesus clearly was defending the innocent party who was put away. Today, the church often takes the role of the Pharisees by condemning the innocent party.

However, the following passage leaves a burning message: "But I say unto you, That whosoever looketh on a woman to lust after her hath committed adultery with her already in his heart" (v. 28, KJV). If we applied this passage even-handedly, every person who has ever looked upon another person other than his or her mate with sexual desire is an adulterer, and therefore disqualified from the ministry and deaconship! Of course, that is not practiced! The fact is clear: adultery can be forgiven. Without a doubt, not a person reading these lines could plead innocent in the face of Jesus' interpretation.

Sexual Unfaithfulness: A Legitimate Cause for Divorce

The Lord Jesus gives the following answer to the Pharisees in their desire to justify their actions against their wives:

> The Pharisees also came to Him, testing Him, and saying to Him, "Is it lawful for a man to divorce his wife for just any reason?" And He answered and said to them, "Have you not read that He who made them at the beginning 'made them male and female,' and said, 'For this reason a man shall leave his father and mother and be joined to his wife, and the two shall become one flesh'? So then, they are no longer two but one flesh. Therefore what God has joined together, let not man separate." They said to Him, "Why then did Moses command to give a certificate of divorce, and to put her away?" He said to them, "Moses, because of the hardness of your hearts, permitted you to divorce your wives, but from the beginning it was not so. And I say to you, whoever divorces his wife, except for sexual immorality, and marries another, commits adultery; and whoever marries her who is divorced commits adultery" (Matthew 19:3-9).

Note the following points:

1. *Jesus affirms God's ideal for marriage.* In the verses above, the Lord appeals to creation and the fact that the sexual union was considered the consummation of marriage. Sexual unfaithfulness was viewed as a type of marriage. Paul affirmed this as well.

Do you not know that your bodies are members of Christ? Shall I then take the members of Christ and make them members of a harlot? Certainly not! Or do you not know that he who is joined to a harlot is one body with her? For "the two," He says, "shall become one flesh." But he who is joined to the Lord is one spirit with Him. Flee sexual immorality. Every sin that a man does is outside the body, but he who commits sexual immorality sins against his own body. Or do you not know that your body is the temple of the Holy Spirit who is in you, whom you have from God, and you are not your own? For you were bought at a price; therefore glorify God in your body and in your spirit, which are God's (1 Corinthians 6:15-20).

2. *Jesus rebukes them for the hardness of their hearts.* As we read earlier, Matthew 19:8 indicated God's displeasure at their callous attitudes.

3. *Jesus gives a valid reason for divorce.* Matthew 19:9 details the guidelines for remarriage. A man commits adultery in remarriage *only* if he divorces his wife for some reason other than unfaithfulness. If she has committed adultery, then he may divorce and remarry. However, the adulterer or adulteress who remarries causes their new mate to commit adultery. The principle is clear: If the innocent party in a divorce (the one not guilty of adultery) remarries, that remarriage is not considered adulterous.

Of course, if adultery occurs in a marriage, divorce should not be automatically pursued. Forgiveness and restoration are possible and should be considered before any divorce. Yet, an innocent mate should realize that a promiscuous partner may be putting his or her own health at risk with so many deadly sexually transmitted diseases rampant in today's society. In cases where a life-threatening lifestyle and perversion are evident, I would encourage divorce.

THOUGHT QUESTIONS

1. What views were taught in your own background regarding the Christian and divorce? About remarriage? About the future of ministry for a leader who has been divorced? What principles or scriptures were these beliefs based on?

2. According to Malachi 2:16, what are God's feelings about divorce?

3. How did the New Testament leaders drift from the Old Testament laws regarding divorce and remarriage? What new light did Jesus shed on divorce, especially regarding lust? What significance does this have on our own qualifications in service for God?

CHAPTER Six

DIVORCE AND REMARRIAGE

PART 2

Divorced persons cannot rebuild their lives on the ashes of ruins. All of the rubble of failure must be swept away and new foundations laid for rebuilding life. This is the task of the church, and one that Spirit-filled leaders will seek to establish in their ministries.

Yet you say, "For what reason?" Because the Lord has been witness between you and the wife of your youth, with whom you have dealt treacherously; yet she is your companion and your wife by covenant. But did He not make them one, having a remnant of the Spirit? And why one? He seeks godly offspring. Therefore take heed to your spirit, and let none deal treacherously with the wife of his youth.

"For the Lord God of Israel says that He hates divorce, for it covers one's garment with violence," says the Lord of hosts. "Therefore take heed to your spirit, that you do not deal treacherously" (Malachi 2:14-16).

Mark's Gospel was written to the Roman culture where women in high places could divorce their husbands. He simply affirms that the principles of Scripture apply to women as well as men. Jesus said, "Whoever divorces his wife and marries another commits adultery against her. And if a woman divorces her husband and marries another, she commits adultery" (10:11, 12).

Luke's Gospel addresses the Pharisees' indiscriminate divorce practices:

> Now the Pharisees, who were lovers of money, also heard all these things, and they derided Him. And He said to them, "You are those who justify yourselves before men, but God knows your hearts. For what is highly esteemed among men is

an abomination in the sight of God. The law and the prophets were until John. Since that time the kingdom of God has been preached, and everyone is pressing into it. And it is easier for heaven and earth to pass away than for one tittle of the law to fail. Whoever divorces his wife and marries another commits adultery; and whoever marries her who is divorced from her husband commits adultery" (16:14-18).

The adultery exception is not mentioned, but it would apply here as well. It is notable in Luke that the Greek for "putting away" is a present active participle. This is a continuous tense that could be better understood as "the one who is repeatedly putting away a wife." Jesus is dealing with the one who has divorced again and again. The word *another* is not the usual *allos* but is the Greek word *heteran*, which means "another of a different kind." Here is a person who has spotted something different that attracts him. His wife is innocent, yet she and her future husband will be stigmatized as adulterers because of the hardness of her adulterer husband.

The second half of verse 18 applies to the promiscuous woman who goes from husband to husband. The presence of the Greek phrase, *ho andros* (translated "her husband"), indicates a woman who was put away for her unfaithfulness. Again, the phrase "commits adultery" is in the continuous tense, indicating many repeated marriages. Thus, habitual offenders are seen as destroyers of God's ideal.

In allowing divorce for the reason of immorality, or illicit sexual intercourse, it is clear that Jesus thought that a person dissolves his marriage by creating a sexual union with someone other than the marriage partner. Such union violates the sacred "oneness" intended by God when he united Adam and Eve in the first marriage relationship (Genesis 2:18-25).

In the case of sexual unfaithfulness, the decree of divorce simply reflects the fact that the marriage has already been broken. A man divorcing his wife for this cause does not "make her an adulteress," for she already is one. Thus, divorce on the grounds of the lack of chastity usually frees the innocent partner to remarry without incurring the guilt of adultery (see Matthew 19:9). However, this is sometimes questioned. Although Jesus allowed divorce for adultery, He did not *require* it. On the contrary, He insisted that divorce disrupts God's plan for marriage, and left the way open for repentance and forgiveness.

Divorce on the Grounds of Abandonment

Paul was in agreement with Jesus' teachings on

marriage and divorce. In the course of his writings, the apostle had to deal with new situations involving marital conflict between two believers and between a believer and a nonbeliever.

In the case of two Christians, Paul admonished them to follow the Lord's teachings and be reconciled. In any event, neither was to marry another (see 1 Corinthians 7:10, 11). In verse 15, Paul wrote that a Christian whose mate has abandoned the marriage should be free to formalize the divorce: "If the unbeliever departs, let him depart; a brother or a sister is not under bondage in such cases." Many authorities hold that the phrase "not under bondage" means that a deserted Christian spouse may lawfully go from divorce to remarriage. But other scholars disagree with this interpretation. In any event, Paul encourages the believer to keep the marriage together in hopes that the unbelieving partner might be saved.

> Now to the married I command, yet not I but the Lord: A wife is not to depart from her husband. But even if she does depart, let her remain unmarried or be reconciled to her husband. And a husband is not to divorce his wife. But to the rest I, not the Lord, say: If any brother has a wife who does not believe, and she is willing to live with him, let him not divorce her. And a woman who has a husband

who does not believe, if he is willing to live with her, let her not divorce him. For the unbelieving husband is sanctified by the wife, and the unbelieving wife is sanctified by the husband; otherwise your children would be unclean, but now they are holy. But if the unbeliever departs, let him depart; a brother or a sister is not under bondage in such cases. But God has called us to peace. For how do you know, O wife, whether you will save your husband? Or how do you know, O husband, whether you will save your wife? (vv. 10-16).

Obviously, the cause for separation in this instance is not adultery. Paul would certainly not contradict the Lord, who allowed the innocent party to remarry. This separation, except for Biblical reasons, does not permit remarriage. Here are the basic Biblical guidelines:

- *For believers.* If two believers separate because of personal differences, not because of adultery or abandonment, then they should make every effort to reconcile. However, if two believers did choose to divorce and then one or both of them remarried someone else, they should not abandon their second marriages to reconcile with their first spouses.

- If one professing Christian spouse abandons another Christian spouse, the spouse who is abandoned should not remarry until the wayward partner remarries or dies. At that point, when there is no longer any hope of reconciliation, then the abandoned believer is free to remarry.

- *For believers married to unbelievers.* In an unequally yoked marriage, if the unbeliever is content to live with a believing spouse, the believer may not divorce the unbeliever. However, should the unbelieving spouse ever leave the union, the believing spouse is released to remarry.

Death Frees Even the Guilty Divorcé to Remarry

The following passage is an illustration about the Law and the fact that the death of Jesus freed believers from the Law. Paul used marriage as a metaphor of this freedom. At death, the surviving partner is free to remarry even if that one has been guilty of adultery.

Or do you not know, brethren (for I speak to those who know the law), that the law has dominion over a man as long as he lives? For the woman who has a husband is bound by the law to her husband as long as he lives. But if the husband dies, she is released from the law of her husband. So then if, while her husband lives, she marries another man, she will be called an adulteress; but if her husband dies, she is free from that law, so that she is no adulteress, though she has married another man (Romans 7:1-3).

Notice that the woman, not the man, was bound

under Jewish law. As we have seen, the Jewish man could divorce almost at will. The phrase "married to another man" implies sexual relations. The word translates from the Greek word *heteros*, which means "of a different kind." If a woman becomes enamored with someone different and lives with that man, she is an adulteress and so is the man (adulterer) she lives with. Of course, this passage applies to the guilty, never the innocent victim of divorce.

Remarriage of One's Former Mate Releases One to Remarry

In the Old Testament, it was an abomination to divorce a current marriage partner in order to return to one's former mate.

> "When a man takes a wife and marries her, and it happens that she finds no favor in his eyes because he has found some uncleanness in her, and he writes her a certificate of divorce, puts it in her hand, and sends her out of his house, when she has departed from his house, and goes and becomes another man's wife, if the latter husband detests her and writes her a certificate of divorce, puts it in her hand, and sends her out of his house, or if the latter husband dies who took her as his wife, then her former husband who divorced her must not take her back to be his wife after she has been defiled; for that is an abomination before the Lord, and you shall not

bring sin on the land which the Lord your God is giving you as an inheritance" (Deuteronomy 24:1-4).

According to the Law, remarriage of one's former mate was viewed the same as death. The bond was irrevocably broken, and the partner was released.

Abuse and Physical Danger Are Grounds for Divorce

In Scripture, laws against battery and murder are clear. Severe penalties were established for even allowing your animals to injure others! Exodus 21:28, 29 outlines those penalties:

> "If an ox gores a man or a woman to death, then the ox shall surely be stoned, and its flesh shall not be eaten; but the owner of the ox shall be acquitted. But if the ox tended to thrust with its horn in times past, and it has been made known to his owner, and he has not kept it confined, so that it has killed a man or a woman, the ox shall be stoned and its owner also shall be put to death."

The Bible deals harshly with the batterer and the potential killer. These criminals forfeit their right to be a part of society, much less lead a family. A woman caught in this situation must protect her life as well as the lives of her children. Over 50 percent of the murders committed in our nation are domestic, related to the family. A person having escaped from such danger would most certainly be free to remarry.

Implications for the Church

1. *Is the innocent party excluded from ministerial or church leadership offices?* Scripture gives no such exclusions. The passage in 1 Timothy 3:1-13 gives us the qualifications for those in ministry:

> This is a faithful saying: If a man desires the position of a bishop, he desires a good work. A bishop then must be blameless, the husband of one wife, temperate, sober-minded, of good behavior, hospitable, able to teach; not given to wine, not violent, not greedy for money, but gentle, not quarrelsome, not covetous; one who rules his own house well, having his children in submission with all reverence (for if a man does not know how to rule his own house, how will he take care of the church of God?); not a novice, lest being puffed up with pride he fall into the same condemnation as the devil. Moreover he must have a good testimony among those who are outside, lest he fall into reproach and the snare of the devil.
>
> Likewise deacons must be reverent, not double-tongued, not given to much wine, not greedy for money, holding the mystery of the faith with a pure conscience. But let these also first be tested; then let them serve as deacons, being found blameless.

Likewise their wives must be reverent, not slan-
derers, temperate, faithful in all things. Let deacons be the husbands of one wife, ruling their children and their own houses well. For those who
have served well as deacons obtain for themselves
a good standing and great boldness in the faith
which is in Christ Jesus.

The whole issue of ordination for ministry is
another study. We do not have any clear teaching on
the ritual of ordination beyond the fact that those set
aside for ministry or missions were given the gift of
"laying on of hands." But a chief issue in church
service is found in the phrase "husband of one
wife," which in the Greek literally translates "of one
woman the man." The passage clearly forbids the
practice of polygamy and the keeping of concubines.
It would forbid a sexually licentious man from service. It would forbid a man from serving who was at
fault in a divorce after his conversion. It would in no
way restrict the innocent man abandoned by an
adulteress wife from serving Christ in ministry. Each
case should be taken individually and decisions for
service determined fairly.

2. *Does it lower some arbitrary standard if divorcés
are included as candidates for ministry or church leadership?* To the contrary, it may raise the standard. You
see in the current arbitrary religious rules of some, a

young man could have been a fornicator with many women and yet never legally married to any of them, become legally married to one woman, repent, and later become a church leader.

At the same time, another man could live faithfully all his life with his wife, only to have her leave with another man, and then find himself excluded from the ministry he feels called to. This is not the teaching of Scripture.

3. *Is a divorced person still married in God's sight to their former mate?* Have you ever heard someone say of a divorced person, "He (or she) has two or more living wives (or husbands)?" Where did such an idea come from? Not from Scripture! Remember the woman at the well:

> The woman answered and said, "I have no husband." Jesus said to her, "You have well said, 'I have no husband,' for you have had five husbands, and the one whom you now have is not your husband; in that you spoke truly" (John 4:17, 18).

The Greek verb *esches*, translated "you *have had* five husbands," is second aorist, the *once and for all* tense in the Greek. These men were no longer her husbands. Divorce dissolves the past relationship.

4. *What are the implications of the terms* blameless *and* reputation *(NIV) in 1 Timothy 3?* The word

blameless translates from the Greek *anegkletos,* which means "that which cannot be called into account, unreprovable, unaccused, blameless." It implies not merely *acquittal,* but the *removal* of even the charge or accusation against a person. The word comes from the court system and implies that the leader must not have a criminal reputation. The innocent party in a divorce is blameless even before the courts.

The ultimate irony must be noted that under some existing religious rules and systems, not even God could be a church leader or pastor!

> Thus says the Lord: "Where is the certificate of your mother's divorce, whom I have put away? Or which of My creditors is it to whom I have sold you? For your iniquities you have sold yourselves, and for your transgressions your mother has been put away" (Isaiah 50:1).

Jehovah divorced Israel and created a new bride, the church. Israel will find her acceptance as she too embraces Christ. Divorce does not contaminate nor does it exclude the innocent from serving. Even the guilty can be forgiven and used by the Lord. The woman at the well who was married five times brought her entire city to Christ. Jesus used her immediately, the very day she was converted.

Therefore, let us conclude that, after careful

examination, a person divorced only once as the innocent party, who meets all the qualifications and has been proven faithful, could serve in a church office as pastor or church leader. The guilty party in a divorce can be forgiven and can go on to serve in many capacities, but not as pastor or in a leadership role within the church.

Divorced persons cannot rebuild their lives on the ashes of ruins. All of the rubble of failure must be swept away and new foundations laid for rebuilding life. This is the task of the church, and one that Spirit-filled leaders will seek to establish in their ministries.

THOUGHT QUESTIONS

1. Look back over the chapter and the passages of Scripture presented. What are three basic grounds for divorce that seem to have Scriptural support? What reasons for divorce are *not* supported by Scripture?

2. What place should forgiveness and reconciliation have for Christians facing difficulties in their marriage? What is the church's responsibility to those who have suffered through the pain of divorce?

Chapter Seven

The Coming Lord

Jesus will come in such power and such glory that, while many may refuse Him, none can deny Him.

Y ou have wearied the Lord with your words; yet you say, "In what way have we wearied Him?" In that you say, "Everyone who does evil is good in the sight of the Lord, and He delights in them," or, "Where is the God of justice?"

"Behold, I send My messenger, and he will prepare the way before Me. And the Lord, whom you seek, will suddenly come to His temple, even the Messenger of the covenant, in whom you delight. Behold, He is coming," says the Lord of hosts.

"But who can endure the day of His coming? And who can stand when He appears? For He is like a refiner's fire and like launderers' soap. He will sit as a refiner and a purifier of silver; He will purify the sons of Levi, and purge them as gold and silver, that they may offer to the Lord an offering in righteousness.

"Then the offering of Judah and Jerusalem will be pleasant to the Lord, as in the days of old, as in former years. And I will come near you for judgment; I will be a swift witness against sorcerers, against adulterers, against perjurers, against those who exploit wage earners and widows and orphans, and against those who turn away an alien — because they do not fear Me," says the Lord of hosts.

"For I am the Lord, I do not change; therefore you are not consumed, O sons of Jacob" (Malachi 2:17 — 3:6).

This passage begins with Malachi boldly telling the people, "You have wearied the Lord with your words" (v. 17). The Lord was weary of the sarcastic questioning of His justice. "Where is the God of justice?" was their blasphemous cry (v. 17). This echoed the age-old atheistic liberal question, "If there is a God, why is there so much trouble in the world?" Down through the years, the same old skepticism has echoed from unbelieving hearts, and according to Peter, we will hear it until Jesus comes:

> Scoffers will come in the last days, walking according to their own lusts, and saying, "Where is the promise of His coming? For since the fathers fell asleep, all things continue as they were from the beginning of creation" (2 Peter 3:3, 4).

Malachi's inspired answer encompasses both the first and second coming of Christ. Often the prophets of the Old Testament viewed the future through the telescope of God's prophetic program and spoke of two great mountain peaks that they saw. These great mountain peaks were the coming of the Lord. And though they seemed to be side by side, they were generations apart. One mountain peak represented the coming of the Lord as the suffering servant; the other represented His coming as the reigning King.

Israel is central in the events of both the first and second coming of the Lord. In Malachi's day, they professed to delight in the prospect of His coming, but in reality, they were not ready for Him to come. The purpose of the coming of the Lord was (and still is) to have a people to be His very own. In doing so, sin must be judged and purged.

The Lord has always been, and still is, spoken of as "the Coming One" (Matthew 11:3; Luke 7:19, 20). To elaborate on what the Bible has to say about the coming of the Lord would take volumes of books, but we will limit our thinking to several things found in this passage that characterize and reveal the eternal purpose of His coming.

He Comes Personally (3:1)

In both the first and second coming, Christ comes to us personally, but the Bible speaks of a "forerunner" (Luke 1:17, *NASB*). The forerunner of the first coming was John the Baptist, who came "in the spirit and power of Elijah" (v. 17). According to Malachi, Elijah will be the forerunner at the second coming of Christ (4:5).

Notice carefully the promise of the One who is coming. The Lord says of the forerunner, "He will prepare the way before Me." Notice also the phrase "the Lord, whom you seek" (3:1). The Hebrew word for *Lord* here is *Adonai*, which means "master." The One who is coming is the Master, the Lord himself. Scripture goes on to say that He will "suddenly come to *His* temple." The owner of the Temple is returning.

The actual identity of the Coming One is revealed as "the Messenger of the covenant" (v. 1). This One is the Giver and Keeper of the covenant. The Messenger, or angel, of the covenant is the Old Testament revelation of the preincarnate Christ. All the Old Testament covenants pointed to the coming of Christ. The Mosaic covenant, confirmed by blood sacrifices, was perfectly fulfilled at the first coming of Christ. The Abrahamic covenant for the land and the Davidic covenant for the throne will be fully and ultimately realized at the second coming of Christ.

The people of Israel were seeking and delighting in the day when the Christ would come, but Malachi warned them that they were not ready. The Coming One is the Lord whom they had not obeyed; the owner of the Temple, the service of which they had despised and desecrated; the Messenger of the covenant they had not kept. There is a message for us here today. Our Lord is coming personally, and we will personally face Him. John says concerning that great event, "And everyone who has this hope in Him purifies himself, just as He is pure" (1 John 3:3). And John also admonished, "And now, little children, abide in Him, that when He appears, we may have confidence and not be ashamed before Him at His coming" (2:28).

He Comes Gloriously (3:2-4)

"But who can endure . . . ? And who can stand when He appears?"

This question emphasizes the power and glory of the Lord. The word *stand* was used to speak of a soldier standing his ground. The question transcends all the years of time to the final judgment, for at the first coming of Jesus, many could not withstand His person of grace, truth and love. During His ministry on earth, many surrendered their lives to Him, but others rejected Him. This is illustrated by the two thieves who died one on each side of Him at Calvary; one believed on Him and the other disbelieved.

At the second coming of Christ, the great host of saints will rejoice at His glorious appearing, then there will be a time during the Great Tribulation when the armies of the Antichrist will gather with the intention of fighting against the saints. But Jesus said concerning that day, "And then shall appear the sign of the Son of man in heaven . . . and they shall see the Son of man coming in the clouds of heaven with power and great glory" (Matthew 24:30, KJV). Paul also said that Christ would come "in flaming fire taking vengeance on those who do not know God" (2 Thessalonians 1:8).

According to Malachi and other writers of Holy Scriptures, every man will behold and acknowledge the glory of the Lord, for ultimately "every knee should bow . . . and . . . every tongue should confess that Jesus Christ is Lord, to the glory of God the Father" (Philippians 2:10, 11). Jesus will come in such power and such glory that, while many may refuse Him, none can deny Him. Malachi states the purpose of the Lord's coming for Israel when he described the Lord as "a refiner's fire" and "launderers' soap" (3:2). The prophet asserts, "As you are right now, you cannot stand when He comes, but He will cleanse and purge many of you, and prepare you for Himself."

In the silver refineries of ancient times, the refiner knew when the metal was pure. As it melted and burned, he would stare into the pot. Suddenly, the silver would lay as still as a mirror, and the refiner could see his own image perfectly and clearly in the pot. When that image was visible, he knew the silver was pure. When Jesus comes and His work in us is finished, we will be like Him, for His blood cleanses from all sin.

He Comes Fearfully (3:5, 6)

The word *judgment* is the Hebrew word *mishpat.* It is used over 400 times in the Old Testament and means "verdict or sentence." The coming of Jesus, both the first and second time, has to do with God's judgment of sin. At His first coming He died, bearing God's judgment of the world upon His own body. All who reject Christ must be judged for their sin at His second coming. If you reject the payment for sin Jesus made for you, you will have to pay for your sin by your eternal torment in hell.

Among the sins Malachi mentioned is sorcery. This refers to the use of the occult and witchcraft and devil worship. It includes the use of potions or drugs and music. Malachi also names adulterers, liars and the unjust as being the objects of the severity of God's judgment. The nature of these sins suggests open defiance of God's law. God said that these individuals have no fear, awe or reverence for Him. In Malachi's day, the people had lost their fear of God, but at the second coming of the Lord, all will bow their knees in reverence to His holiness.

There is forgiveness with the Lord, and security in Him. He will gather His people for Himself and for His glory. If you do not know Him who has come and who will come again, call upon Him now. Rest upon His death on the cross as payment for your sin, and He will save you and receive you to Himself.

Thought Questions

1. Have you ever been asked the question, "If God is so good, why does He allow so much evil in the world?" How did you respond?

2. The nation of Israel was excited about the coming of the Messiah and claimed to be looking for Him, but they weren't preparing for His return. How is this like the church today? What should we be doing personally and corporately to be ready for Christ's coming?

3. What was mentioned as the purpose of both the first and second coming of Christ? How does this purpose motivate the way you live your Christian life and ministry?

CHAPTER EIGHT

THIEVES IN
GOD'S HOUSE

Tithing is a timeless principle for living.

"Yet from the days of your fathers you have gone away from My ordinances and have not kept them. Return to Me, and I will return to you," says the Lord of hosts. "But you said, 'In what way shall we return?'

"Will a man rob God? Yet you have robbed Me! But you say, 'In what way have we robbed You?' In tithes and offerings. You are cursed with a curse, for you have robbed Me, even this whole nation. Bring all the tithes into the storehouse, that there may be food in My house, and try Me now in this," says the Lord of hosts, "if I will not open for you the windows of heaven and pour out for you such blessing that there will not be room enough to receive it.

"And I will rebuke the devourer for your sakes, so that he will not destroy the fruit of your ground, nor shall the vine fail to bear fruit for you in the field," says the Lord of hosts; and all nations will call you blessed, for you will be a delightful land," says the Lord of hosts.

"Your words have been harsh against Me," says the Lord, "yet you say, 'What have we spoken against You?' You have said, 'It is useless to serve God; what profit is it that we have kept His ordinance, and that we have walked as mourners before the Lord of hosts? So now we call the proud blessed, for those who do wickedness are raised up; they even tempt God and go free'" (Malachi 3:7-15).

In verse 8, Malachi asks the question, "Will a man rob God?" This word *rob* is the Hebrew *qaba,* which implies premeditated thievery by force. In this passage, God clearly states there were thieves in His house.

It is unthinkable that a person would rob the benevolent and generous heavenly Father, but there is a greater disaster revealed in these verses. The people were disobeying the Lord, and God's blessings were shut off. The very means of their prosperity had been forsaken! Their faithfulness to keep God's ordinances would have kept that channel of His blessing open.

Malachi reveals for us a secret of revival and prosperity. God called on His people to return to Him, then promised that He would return to them.

"In what way shall we return?" they asked. The Lord reminded them of their departure from His ordinances and that, in departing, they had robbed Him. It was made plain that a return to the ordinances was a return to the Lord. For the curse to be lifted, they had to return to the ordinance of tithes and offerings. The channel had to be cleared for the windows of heaven to be opened.

Is this not the secret of revival today? When there is confession of the sins of disobedience and a return to the principles of God's Word, the channel is opened to receive God's favor and power. We must return to the principle of tithing. To tithe is to give 10 percent of your income to God. It is vital to one's spiritual health and general prosperity. To keep the tithe to yourself is to invoke God's curse on you, your family, your church and our nation. This passage teaches three vital truths that relate tithing to heaven.

Tithing Obeys Heaven

To tithe is to obey a specific command of God. The practice of tithing came before the giving of the Law. According to Genesis and Hebrews, Abraham was the first to pay tithes in the Old Testament. Genesis 14:17-24 records the account of Abraham refusing the reward of the king of Sodom and receiving communion from the hand of the king-priest of Salem, Melchizedek. Upon the pronunciation of a blessing on Abraham by Melchizedek, Abraham gave him tithes of all he had.

Jacob's first vow after his wondrous vision of heaven was to become a tither (see Genesis 28:20-22). Under the Law, tithing was instituted in Leviticus 27:30-33:

> And all the tithe of the land, whether of the seed of the land or of the fruit of the tree, is the Lord's. It is holy to the Lord. If a man wants at all to redeem any of his tithes, he shall add one-fifth to it. And concerning the tithe of the herd or the flock, of whatever passes under the rod, the tenth one shall be holy to the Lord. He shall not inquire whether it is good or bad, nor shall he exchange it; and if he exchanges it at all, then both it and the one exchanged for it shall be holy; it shall not be redeemed.

Tithes were used to pay the priests and to maintain the house of worship. Every third year, the tithes were used to feed the people in a feast to Jehovah (see Deuteronomy 26:12, 13). If a man could not make the journey to Jerusalem, he invited a Levite (one from the priestly line) to his home for a feast, using the tithe. Tithing was to be a blessing to the giver also (see Deuteronomy 14:24-27).

In the New Testament, tithing is advocated and endorsed. Jesus commended the Pharisees for tithing, while He rebuked them for omitting mercy. The New Testament indicates that believers gave *more* than a tithe! Not only were offerings made, but believers also made available to God everything they owned.

History affirms the Biblical record. Origen, Jerome and Chrysostom taught and practiced tithing in the early church. Tithing was recognized as early as A.D. 786 in England. King Alfred, Edgar and Canute were all tithers. In 1545, the Council of Trent enjoined tithing to all the church, and threatened to discipline all who refused to do so.

Tithing is a timeless principle for living. Some argue that we are no longer obligated to tithe, because it was part of the Law. Despite the fact that tithing was first commanded in Mosaic Law, the principle was established and stood before the Law, and it still stands today. Just because we are not under the law for salvation does not remove our obligation to obey the law for sanctification. The Law Giver and Law Keeper lives in the heart of every believer, and He advocates the principle.

Tithing Opens Heaven

Dr. Stephen Olford declared that Malachi 3:10 teaches the proper *proportion* of giving (10%), the proper *place* to give (the "storehouse" or the church), and the proper *purpose* of tithing—"that there may be food in My house." God's house can be fully provided for through His people.

When God's children are faithful in tithing, God proves Himself faithful. He opens the windows of heaven and pours out blessings so great they cannot be contained or measured. These blessings may be material, spiritual, personal or national. God says that giving is the means to which He responds with blessing. Understand, tithing does not guarantee prosperity to the point of making you wealthy in a material way. An act of obedience to God enables Him to lift the curse and to provide for us according to all our needs.

Tithing is a universal principle. A number of years ago in the Philippines, I visited a fine deacon of the Dueling Baptist Church. He lived in a modest, but nice, home. Around his home, I noticed an abundance of rice and cattle. In conversation with this man, I learned that he was a faithful tither, and then I understood why his harvest was so great that he had no place to store it all. He sold much of it, and gave the money to the Lord. He had the habit of giving every pastor in the area a 100-pound sack of rice. I was so moved by what I witnessed in the example of this dear man that I gave away everything I took with me except the clothes needed to wear home. God opens heaven for those who obey Him.

Tithing Obligates Heaven

When we are obedient to the Lord in tithing, God promises to do two things in response to our obedience:

1. *Protect our work* (v. 11). The Lord says, "And I will rebuke the devourer for your sakes." In Malachi's day, vandals would often destroy crops and vineyards. Satan is the devourer we have to contend with. He destroys people and property, peace and power, provision and protection. Obedience to God brings His authoritative rebuke against this destruction.

2. *Project our witness* (v. 12). *Blessed* and *delightful* are the words used to describe God's obedient people in this verse. God's blessing upon us makes us attractive to the unsaved. It strengthens our testimony and makes us refreshing to those around us. By giving our resources together, we are able to do as a church what we are not able to do as individuals. We can project our witness around the world. This

is what the Lord had in mind when He said, "That there may be food in My house" (v. 10).

Years ago in Scotland, Archbishop William Temple was leading the church in worship, with the hymn "When I Survey the Wondrous Cross." As they were about to sing the last stanza, Dr. Temple asked the people to pause long enough to read it before they sang it. Their voices became almost a whisper as they were overtaken and subdued by the depth of the words they sang:

> Were the whole realm of nature mine,
> That were a present far too small;
> Love so amazing, so divine,
> Demands my soul, my life, my all!

Perhaps you too will express your determination to be an obedient servant, no matter the cost, just as did this poet:

> Ah, when I look up at that cross,
> When God's great steward suffered loss;
> Yea, life and blood for me!
> A trifling thing it seems to be,
> To pay the tithe, dear Lord, to Thee,
> Of time or talent, wealth or store;
> Full well I know, I owe Thee more!
> A million times I owe Thee more!
> But that is just the reason why

I lift my heart to God on high,
And pledge Thee by this portion small,
My life, my love, my all in all!
This holy token at Thy cross,
I know, as money, must seem but dross;
But in my heart, Lord, thou wouldst see
How it has pledged my all to Thee,
That I a steward true must be.

— Ralph Cushman

THOUGHT QUESTIONS

1. What is the result of keeping the commanded tithe to yourself? What is the outcome of following God's command and giving Him 10 percent of your increase?

2. Some would argue that tithing is an Old Testament principle that was under the Law and, therefore, no longer applies to us. What New Testament principles in this chapter indicate otherwise?

3. Have you ever made excuses about holding back your tithe? Examine your giving record and ask God to show you how to be a faithful and obedient steward with the resources He gives you. Write out your commitment to be faithful.

Chapter Nine

GOD'S JEWEL
BOX

Let's talk about Jesus; the King of kings is He,
The Lord of lords supreme, through all eternity,
The great I AM, the way, the truth, the life, the door;
Let's talk about Jesus more and more.

*T*hen those who feared the Lord spoke to one another, and the Lord listened and heard them; so a book of remembrance was written before Him for those who fear the Lord and who meditate on His name.

"They shall be Mine," says the Lord of hosts, "On the day that I make them My jewels. And I will spare them as a man spares his own son who serves him." Then you shall again discern between the righteous and the wicked, between one who serves God and one who does not serve Him" (Malachi 3:16-18).

When I was in seminary, I knew a teaching fellow named Jerry Perrald. Jerry eventually went to Cambodia as a foreign missionary, and I've lost track of him over the years, but I knew and admired him then as an excellent scholar in terms of Hebrew, Greek and theology. He liked to have meetings or gatherings at his house with preachers and their wives.

We didn't eat at these gatherings, except perhaps a cup of hot tea, as Jerry was British-born. Inevitably, we would turn to the Scriptures in those days. All of us attending those home meetings were working two jobs—as a church pastor and some other side job while trying to complete our education. In spite of our schedules, one night a week we often met until after midnight as we reverenced the Word of God, prayed and sang old hymns. As I reflect on those days, I sense God saying, "I was pleased when you did that."

We have come to think of worship as something formal. But worship is a lifestyle! It should be who we are and what we do. Augustine was right when he said, "Our hearts are restless until they rest in Thee." There is something in us that drives us to seek after God.

The Book of Malachi records two different strains of conversation in Israel. Most of the book is taken up with the *discordant* voices giving expression of displeasure, distrust and disgust. The conversation of these people is filled with their criticism and complaining. In the closing part of the book, Malachi turns his attention to the *desirable* voices of a remnant of people who remained faithful. Their conversation reflected their disposition to love the glorious name of God, the very opposite of the disgruntled people Malachi addressed in 1:6-8.

Malachi acknowledged that these people feared the Lord (4:2). The name that they reverenced was *Yahweh*, known also as the great "I AM." Their reverence of the Lord was the basis for their relationship with each other. Malachi says of their conversation, "They spoke often to one another" (see 3:16). These people who loved the Lord were individuals who were not all alike, but they met together with others who reverenced the Lord. They were friends who lifted up their God as the subject of their conversations.

Furthermore, we are told that they "meditate[d] on His name" (v. 16). The Hebrew word for *meditate* (*thought,* KJV) is *chashab,* which means "to focus one's mind on something of great value." This remnant of faithful people valued one thing above all else: the name of Yahweh. This name represented His character, which they held in awe. That fear of His name prompted their unwavering service to Him.

If somebody listened in on your conversation, even with your buddies, what would they hear? From some of you they would hear about your aches and pains. "Nobody has a boil that hurts as bad as mine." Sadly, perhaps someone would overhear dirty jokes from some of you. Others may repent inane conversation about things that don't amount to a hill of beans and mean nothing in the light of eternity — like baseball scores and celebrity gossip. What do we talk about when we sit around with our friends? Do we see a "day off" as a day off from God?

The Lord makes four wonderful promises to those who serve Him and reverence His name in word and in thought.

I Will Regard You (v. 16)

"The Lord listened and heard them."

The faithful people of God have the ear of the Almighty! The psalmist said, "The eyes of the Lord are on the righteous, and His ears are open to their cry" (34:15). There is power in the praise of the saints. Scripture indicates that God inhabits the praises of His people. In public assembly and in private worship, we need to speak of the goodness and glory of the Lord. We have His full attention when we do!

I Will Remember You (v. 16)

"A book of remembrance was written before Him."

The Lord is keeping a record of those who serve Him in faithfulness. We know that the ancient Persian monarchs kept books of the good deeds of their people. In Esther 6, we find King Ahasuerus reading such a book one sleepless night. That book had recorded the fact that a man named Mordecai had once saved the king's life. This is probably the concept that Malachi's "book of remembrance" came from.

God will not forget those who serve Him faithfully. David knew this and wrote, "You number my wanderings; put my tears into Your bottle; are they not in Your book?" (Psalm 56:8). Oh, blessed thought! He knows and cares about His people. Are you faithful to Him? He will never forget you! Regardless of your culture or color, your social standing, your lack of prominence or popularity, God knows you and will never forget you.

I Will Reward You (v. 17)

"They shall be Mine . . . on the day that I make them My jewels."

This verse is full of wonderful blessings. It describes God's people under four relationships:

1. *God's Property*—"They shall be Mine." God's stamp of ownership is upon all who have given their lives to Him. Paul said, "You are not your own; you were bought at a price" (1 Corinthians 6:19, 20, *NIV*). "Nevertheless the solid foundation of God stands, having this seal: The Lord knows those who are His" (2 Timothy 2:19).

2. *God's Treasure*—"My jewels." God has placed a high value on His people. The word *make* used in

Malachi 3:17 is a translation of the Hebrew word *asah,* which, in reference to God, speaks of "creative activity." Basically, God has made us as a treasure! Our worth is the value He places on us.

As we meditate more on this passage, it is sobering to comprehend that the Lord is listening to our conversation. Our private worship not only brings joy to Him, but it also makes us more effective. You will find that when you play praise music in the background and start reading the Word of God, praying and talking about Jesus, creative impulses begin to rise in you from the Holy Ghost! You will find you have what you need to help you get through trials.

The word *jewel* is the translation of another Hebrew word, *segullah,* which refers to a "movable treasure." It has the connotation of a private, special treasure like a fine jewel, carried around by its owner. This is the word used to describe Israel as they entered the Mosaic covenant (see Exodus 19:5). It is used repeatedly in the Pentateuch to describe Israel, referring to a "peculiar people" (KJV) or a "special people." The New Testament continues the concept in Titus 2:14 and 1 Peter 2:9. We should not fail to put our minds firmly on the fact of our immense worth to God.

3. *God's Sons*—"as a man spares his own son." This alludes to the family relationship. A good

father will always have a special place in his heart for his own sons. The Bible teaches that the saved are the sons of God by faith. Paul said, "And because you are sons, God has sent forth the Spirit of His Son into your hearts, crying out, Abba, Father!" (Galatians 4:6). The presence of the Holy Spirit in our hearts gives us the sense of the blessed father/son relationship. We are enabled to own Him as Father because He has received us as sons. This is true only of the redeemed.

4. *God's Servants*—"one who serves God." It is a special privilege to be numbered among the servants of God. One of the tragedies revealed in the parable of the prodigal son is that the young man lost his place of service. He could not serve his father while in the far country. The faithful in the family of God know the joy of having the position of servitude, and what joy the servant brings to the Father.

I Will Rescue You (vv. 17, 18)

"And I will spare them."

In the next chapter, the day of a burning terror is described. That day will also be a time of protection and reward for God's faithful people. When the Lord said through the prophet, "I will spare them," He promised to rescue them from out of the great day of His wrath. This promise has a twofold prophetic implication. There was a preservation and a sparing of a remnant who looked for the first coming of Christ; there will be a sparing of the church at the second coming of Christ. At His appearing and before the Tribulation, the saints will be taken out of this world. God will rescue His church from the time of Jacob's Trouble, known as the Tribulation period, when God will pour out His wrath upon this earth.

God has set a difference between the lost and the saved, the righteous and the unrighteous. The believer is not destined to feel God's wrath, according to 1 Thessalonians 5. God will refine and build the great treasure — His people — but they will be rescued and spared from His wrath.

Are you one of God's jewels? You can say every name you want to name, but "there is no other name under heaven given among men by which we must be saved" (Acts 4:12). If we could just sit down a little while and talk, I would want to tell you about Jesus, because sooner or later, if you are around me, we've got to get around to that conversation. I would be on my way to hell if it wasn't for Him. I'm no good except through Him and in His righteousness. I have nothing better to talk about than Jesus Christ.

We used to sing a little chorus:

Let's talk about Jesus; the King of kings is He,
The Lord of lords supreme, through all eternity,
The great I AM, the way, the truth, the life, the door;
Let's talk about Jesus more and more.

THOUGHT QUESTIONS

1. Malachi addressed two different groups of people in Israel—one group was known for their discordant, complaining voices, and the other group had the desirable spirit and attitudes that pleased God. With which of these two groups would Malachi identify *you* in today's church? Does your life and conversation bring pleasure to the heart of God?

2. God makes four promises to those who reverence His name: His regard, His remembrance, His reward and His rescue. What would each of these benefits mean for you? How would the promise of His attention and focus on you transform your prayer life?

3. As God's child, you are His jewel, His "movable treasure" He carries with Him. Do you fully embrace the truth of your immense worth to Him?

CHAPTER
TEN

THE BURNING
HELL

The only place of safety and security is in Christ. The Bible states, "There is therefore now no condemnation to those who are in Christ Jesus" (Romans 8:1).

"*For behold, the day is coming, burning like an oven, and all the proud, yes, all who do wickedly will be stubble. And the day which is coming shall burn them up,*" says the Lord of hosts, "*That will leave them neither root nor branch*" (Malachi 4:1).

We should view these final verses of Malachi with great solemnity. The word *behold* here means "to watch out or study intensely." Malachi 4 sets in contrast the two possible destinies of man. One destiny is the burning judgment of God; the other is the sunrise of a new world. It is interesting that both the Old and the New Testament end with a declaration of the two final states of humanity.

This passage denies the teaching of *universalism*, which states that ultimately all men will be saved. The passage also refutes *liberalism*, which contends that there is no hell. In addition, *humanism* is torn apart, with its false contention that man can perfect himself. *Atheism* is also rejected, for it states that there is no God or afterlife.

The Bible reveals three great periods that may be called *days*. The time before Jesus was a *day of guilt*. The time since the death and resurrection of Jesus is called *the day of grace*. Sometime in the future, known only to God, the day of grace will give way to *the Day of the Lord*. This will be the day that climaxes all of history, brings to an end all world systems, and establishes the reign of Christ as King of kings and Lord of lords. All the unsaved will face the terror of the Great White Throne Judgment. The Day of the Lord will be the beginning of eternal grief and doom for the unsaved. This one verse gives us three truths about that terrible day.

It Is a Future Day

Through the centuries, many dark shadows have fallen across this sin-cursed planet. In the days of Noah, God sent the Flood and all but eight souls perished. It was a dark day when fire and brimstone destroyed southern Israel and its leading cities, Sodom and Gomorrah. The kingdom of Babylon, said to be invincible, experienced a time of darkness when the hand of God wrote upon the wall an announcement of impending judgment. Darkness engulfed the land of Israel when the Roman army marched in by the thousands, leaving death and destruction in its path. What an awful day it was when the bubonic plague took the lives of 30 million people in Europe! And there are many living today who vividly remember the dark clouds of destruction during World Wars I and II that took the lives of so many.

However, the darkest day of all is still ahead for an unredeemed world. According to Malachi, that day of retribution is certain, for he says twice in this verse that "the day is coming." Just as surely as the sun rises in the east, that day is on its way and this world is closer to His return with each passing day. Where will you be in that future day? The only place of safety and security is in Christ. The Bible states, "There is therefore now no condemnation to those who are in Christ Jesus" (Romans 8:1).

It Is a Fearful Day

Malachi uses two images related to fire to describe the destruction of that terrible day. First, he speaks of a burning oven toward which the unrighteous are headed. The second image is that of a wild fire sweeping across a field, and the wicked are as mere stubble in the unstoppable flames.

Malachi was the last of the prophets, before John the Baptist, to herald the coming of Jesus. His message agrees with that of the prophets of the Old Testament, which was given in many passages (see Isaiah 10:16; 30:27; Jeremiah 21:11-14; Joel 2:1-3; Zephaniah 1:14-18). When you read these verses and then study the New Testament, a terrifying picture of burning judgment emerges. A solemn warning of a fiery judgment against willful sinners is clear.

Jesus spoke of a "fire that is not quenched" (see Mark 9:43-48). He told the story of the rich man who cried out from hell, "I am tormented in this flame" (Luke 16:24). He talked to His disciples about the burning of the tares at the end of the age (see Matthew 13:24-30, 36-42). Paul also wrote of this truth when he said, "The Lord Jesus is revealed from heaven with His mighty angels, in flaming fire taking vengeance on those who do not know God, and on those who do not obey the gospel of our Lord Jesus Christ" (2 Thessalonians 1:7, 8). In Revelation, accounts of God's judgment are given that speak of fire falling from heaven upon this sin-cursed earth (8:7, 8; 13:13; 20:9). It is recorded that after the Great White Throne Judgment, those who reject Christ will be bound and cast into the lake of fire (21:8).

Again, consider the question, "Where will you be on that day?" I recall a song my church sang years ago about that day of fire:

> Oh, my loving brother,
> When the world's on fire,
> Don't you want God's bosom
> To be your pillow?
> Hide me over in the Rock of Ages,
> Rock of Ages, hide thou me!

It Is a Final Day

These closing words of Malachi 4:1 are filled with the sadness of a great tragedy. God says that He will destroy both "root and branch." When God destroys one's root, He removes his history and heritage in a complete obliteration. All his life is utterly forgotten—all awards, accomplishments and acclaims. In hell there is no past, nothing from which to draw satisfaction. There are no good memories to recall, only retribution for sin.

In destroying the "branch," that person's future is bleak. Because of their rejection of the Savior, people are cut off, separated from God. They cannot produce spiritually. In this life there is still opportunity for people to repent and come to Christ for salvation. As they do, they are given the capacity to reproduce themselves spiritually. However, those who reject the Savior are finally cut off and cast into hell, where the only productivity is the eternal retribution for sin. The lost in hell have no future, no possible hope.

In the epic poem titled *Inferno,* Dante paints a graphic picture of the levels of hell. Dante imagines nine levels in hell, with the lowest level reserved for liars. While his theology was weak and even some imagery primitive, his picture of what was written over the door of hell strikes every person who reads this powerful poem: "Abandon all hope, ye who enter in." The great day of judgment is indeed eternal and final!

Now the question is, Who will face that fearful and final judgment? Malachi leaves no room for speculation. He names them: "all the proud, yes, all who do wickedly." The word *proud* in Hebrew means "to boil over." Malachi spoke of those self-sufficient people as bubbling over with self-justification and self-righteousness. Their wickedness was literal confusion and restlessness. In their rebellion against God, wicked people may appear to be calm. But as Isaiah said, they are "like the troubled sea, when it cannot rest, whose waters cast up mire and dirt" (57:20).

Oh, my friend, if you are without Christ, you are not self-sufficient. You cannot save yourself. You will not be spared by your self-righteousness. You don't feel any peace now, and you face an endless time of restlessness and suffering in the fires of God's judgment. Turn to God today by putting your faith in the death of Jesus for your sin. The Bible says, "For whoever calls on the name of the Lord shall be saved" (Romans 10:13). He is waiting for you to call upon Him right now.

Thought Questions

1. The reality of hell and judgment is clearly presented in Scripture, and emphasized by the final words of both the Old and New Testaments. Yet many pastors and teachers avoid addressing this somber subject. How many sermons have you heard in the past year on the topic of eternal punishment? In the past 10 years? Does your pastor receive criticism for preaching this topic?

2. Have you ever been through a time of intense terror? Perhaps you have memories of living through World War II, the Vietnam crisis or a time of serious personal tragedy? Or, like many Americans, were you struck by fear as the events of September 11, 2001, unfolded? It is easy for us as Christians to avoid thinking at length about the coming terror for those who will experience end-time events, perhaps due to our personal security in our salvation in Christ. However, we must not forget the terror that awaits unbelievers, so that we strive to warn them while we have time.

3. Take time to make a list of those in your life that you know need Christ. Commit to pray daily for those on your list, and ask God for opportunities to share your faith in love and honesty.

CHAPTER ELEVEN

SUNRISE TOMORROW

The Sun of Righteousness will arise with healing in His wings. There is a divine covering of health, a divine promise, and that promise is rooted in prayer.

"*But to you who fear My name the Sun of Righteousness shall arise with healing in His wings; and you shall go out and grow fat like stall-fed calves. You shall trample the wicked, for they shall be ashes under the soles of your feet on the day that I do this," says the Lord of hosts.*

"Remember the Law of Moses, My servant, which I commanded him in Horeb for all Israel, with the statutes and judgments. Behold, I will send you Elijah the prophet before the coming of the great and dreadful day of the Lord. And he will turn the hearts of the fathers to the children, and the hearts of the children to their fathers, lest I come and strike the earth with a curse" (Malachi 4:2-6).

T hough the coming of the Lord is the sunset of a sin-scarred world, it is a glorious sunrise for a new one. As we examine Malachi 4:2-6, we find some wonderful truths of instruction, challenge and comfort.

Believers today are living in the Elijah generation. Scripture seems to indicate that there were three manifestations of Elijah that appeared after the great prophet's death. One happened in John the Baptist. The spirit of Elijah was upon him, and he heralded the first coming of Jesus. Second, the Bible says that in the last days after the coming of Christ, during the Tribulation, two prophets will come. Most scholars agree that these prophets will be Moses and Elijah.

According to Malachi, there appears to be a third

manifestation of Elijah indicated. This third group represents the same Holy Spirit that filled Elijah and will prophetically prepare the world for the coming of Jesus. I announce to you that you and I, as the end-time church, are part of the Elijah generation! We have the high privilege of representing our Lord to the ends of the earth.

Since the Bible is the inerrant Word of God, it is no surprise that the Old Testament and New Testament end the same. If you go to the end of the Book of Revelation, you will find a warning about hell, a beautiful picture of heaven and an invitation to make your choice. And in Malachi, we find the same thing! We discover an important calling upon our lives as members of the Elijah generation. We have some truths to herald to the world.

A New Depth

"But to you who fear My name . . . "

This word *fear* in the original Hebrew means "you who reverence or count My name as holy." One of the Ten Commandments was "You shall not take the name of the Lord your God in vain" (Deuteronomy 5:11). We have often thought this commandment refers to merely cursing out of our mouth, but it means that and more. If you say His name and don't enter into what He has promised, you have made His name empty. If in your life you are confessing His name, but His name's power is not being released in your life, you have taken the name of the Lord your God in vain.

There is such depth to the name of God! The Hebrew names for Yahweh hold great significance. In verse 3 of this final chapter of Malachi, we see He is the "Lord of hosts," which is the same as Lord of Sabaoth. That means He is King of angels, King of the heavenly hosts!

In verse 2, we go on to read, "[He is] the Sun of Righteousness." This refers to Jehovah-Tsidkenu, as we have no righteousness of our own. He arises "with healing." He is Jehovah-Rophe, your healer. "You shall go out and grow fat." That phrase isn't a reference to size, it is a synonym for prosperity! He is Jehovah-Jireh, your provider. He will feed you. "You shall trample the wicked." He is Jehovah-Nissi, your banner that leads you into battle.

Through all the chapters of Malachi, we find many more examples of the revelation of God's name. Through them all, we hear God clearly saying, "I'm looking for some people who will reverence My name." The Elijah generation, the last days' generation, is going to be a people who understand that

He is our only righteousness. He is our healer. He leads us to victory. He is the Lord of hosts!

A New Day

When the end of the age comes, it is sunset if you are not saved, but it is sunrise for all who know Him. It is a brand-new beginning for everyone who will open his or her heart. Psalm 84:11 says, "The Lord God is a sun and shield; the Lord will give grace and glory; no good thing will He withhold from those who walk uprightly."

What does it mean when Scripture says, "He is the Sun"? Of course, this does not mean He is literally the great ball of flame that heats our earth. He made that sun, and before early scientists even had figured it out, He knew the sun was the center of our solar system and that everything would revolve around that sun. However, as our Sun of Righteousness, He is the center of life. He is the Light of the World, and every day with Him is a new day!

It may have been dark when you got up this morning. Your life may look like it is the end of something, but He is the Sun of Righteousness. He is the giver of a new beginning!

A New Dimension

"The Sun of Righteousness shall arise with healing in His wings."

In God's Word, we find at least three other references to wings that have healing in their wake. One is in Isaiah 40:31: "Those who wait on the Lord shall renew their strength; they shall mount up with wings like eagles, they shall run and not be weary, they shall walk and not faint."

The first thing a doctor may tell you to do when you get sick is to rest! When you catch a cold virus, you can take every prescription or over-the-counter medication, or you can drink orange juice and load up with 2,000 units of vitamin C. However, you aren't going to get well for four or five days unless you rest and allow God to heal you. Sometimes His healing is simply a renewal of your body.

Reflecting on Elijah, we see that was what was wrong with him.

- He had fought spiritual battles.

- He fought Jezebel, a wicked queen.

- He killed the 800 prophets.

Following these amazing victories, though, he suddenly felt fear and ran from Jezebel. He collapsed under a juniper tree because he was just absolutely worn out. It wasn't demons. It was just physical and emotional fatigue (see 2 Kings 19).

There is a healing in waiting and being renewed. That's why we need vacation and rest time. No matter how much you love your routine, you need a change of pace and a time to refresh your spirit. Even Jesus said to His disciples, "Come aside . . . and rest a while" (Mark 6:31).

Psalm 91 begins, "He who dwells in the secret place of the Most High shall abide under the shadow of the Almighty." Verse 4 goes on to say, "Under His wings you shall take refuge." There is a healing that takes place before you even can get sick.

A movie was released in 2002 called *Minority Report*. The premise involved the main characters using advanced technology to look into the future and arrest a criminal long before he committed a crime, thus preventing the crime from ever occurring. This reminds us of another way God heals—by preventing sickness from coming into our lives. Read Psalm 91. The pestilence that stalks at night and the diseases that move in the darkness cannot live where the Sun of Righteousness abides. Have you ever said, "I don't know that I've ever had a major healing"? When you get to heaven, you may discover how many close calls you had and how many times God

Almighty stepped in to bless you and to help you!

We also find healing wings in reference to the cherubim whose wings arch over the bloody mercy seat in the Holy of Holies. That represents an intimacy with God, which is so powerful that disease cannot stay. As Isaiah said, "By His stripes we are healed" (53:5). Can you imagine getting beyond the veil and getting under those wings of the covering of Almighty God on that mercy seat? You can live under those wings!

In Hebrew, the word *wings* is the same word used for the Jewish prayer shawl. The Jewish *taleif*, or prayer shawl, literally pictured the wings of God! This tells us that when you pray, the wings of heaven cover you.

We must absorb this great truth and spread its message to others. The Sun of Righteousness will arise with healing in His wings. There is a divine covering of health, a divine promise, and that promise is rooted in prayer.

A New Dynamic

We have a unique privilege of spreading the wings of God and His covering over our generation. The system God set in place to do this is through the local church.

Many Christians never actually get around to joining a church. They float from one to another, finding spiritual food "on the run," never settling in to a place of family and service. If you are not in a local church, there is no covering over you. It doesn't matter what label is on the front of the church; if it is a New Testament church that believes the Bible is truth, embraces sound doctrine, and believes in the life-saving blood of Jesus, then it comes with a promise of God's covering.

Malachi writes, "Remember the Law of Moses . . . which I commanded him in Horeb" (4:4). Mount Horeb is Mount Sinai in Arabia, present-day Saudi Arabia. Anytime we see Horeb in Scripture, we are to be reminded of more than just the Ten Commandments. It involves the totality of what God did there. It was there Moses saw the glory of God in the burning bush (Exodus 3:1). It was at Horeb that water came from out of the rock (17:6). At Horeb, God set forth the blood covenant (see 2 Chronicles 5:10; Malachi 4:4). Also, Horeb was the place where Moses interceded for the sinning nation that had bowed down before the golden calf (Deuteronomy 9:8). Moses begged God, "Please, Yahweh, save them and send me to hell in their place." God saw a foreshadowing of His Son, Jesus

Christ, in Moses the prophet and spared the people.

As the Elijah generation, we must become so desperate for souls that we are willing to stand up and say:

> Lord, whatever it costs, whatever it takes, we want to get the gospel to the ends of the earth! We're not afraid of any man-made power. We aren't fearful of a militant Islam. We're not afraid of a dead religiosity. We're not afraid of a scorching paganism. We've got the good news! Spare them, Lord. Save them, Lord!

There is a tomorrow for all who know Jesus. There is no tomorrow for the unsaved. Oh, how we who know His mercy look forward to the picture painted by these words:

> The heavens shall glow with splendor,
> But brighter far than they
> The saints shall shine in glory,
> As Christ shall them array;
> The beauty of the Savior,
> Shall dazzle every eye,
> In the crowning day that's coming
> By and by.
>
> Our pain shall then be over,
> We'll sin and sigh no more.
> Behind us all of sorrow,
> And naught but joy before,

A joy in our Redeemer,
As we to Him are nigh,
In the crowning day that's coming
By and by.

— Anonymous

THOUGHT QUESTIONS

1. We have a responsibility to represent God's name to the world. What aspects of His name do you reflect? His peace? His healing? His protection? How can your daily life mirror His character?

2. God's wings of protection and rest can shelter us in these last days as we await His return. How have you experienced the wings of His covering? Have you shared these experiences with others in order to enrich their own faith?

3. Why is it important for believers to be under the covering of a local church in this Elijah generation? What protection and blessings come to those who fellowship with the body of Christ?

CHAPTER
TWELVE

WORDS FOR AN
ELIJAH GENERATION

Let us look ahead with joy and gladness to the hope of the coming of Christ, but not fail in our responsibility to this generation that desperately needs the overwhelming grace of God!

"I am the Lord, I do not change . . ." (Malachi 3:6).

"Jesus Christ is the same yesterday, today, and forever" (Hebrews 13:8).

Throughout the pages of this study, we have learned that God's Word is forever relevant, even when it teaches about past history. God is consistent! "I am the Lord, I do not change . . ." (Malachi 3:6). "Jesus Christ is the same yesterday, today, and forever" (Hebrews 13:8).

Our Creator has a consistency with which He governs the universe. The principles that were true in Malachi as the curtain dropped on the Old Testament still stand true as we near the end of this age.

God would be silent in spoken word for 400 years after Malachi penned his short book. God would tell the people clearly that He would speak to them again. The last of the prophets would actually be John the Baptist, who would come in the Spirit and power of Elijah. He would herald God's final word to man: Jesus Christ.

Malachi showed us the failures of government and religion that always mark coming judgment. What Malachi saw then is consistent with what we see today! But Malachi made an unusual promise as we discussed in the last chapter — a promise of the coming of an "Elijah" before the end of time. Could it be that the prophet Elijah, who came historically during the reign of Ahab and Jezebel, and then whose spirit and message was demonstrated by John the Baptist, is yet to come?

Prophecy buffs would immediately say yes. Elijah is of course listed in New Testament prophecy as one of the two Tribulation period witnesses of Revelation 11. With this I totally agree. But there is more!

Elijah Here Today!

In Matthew 17, Jesus uttered a strange prophecy about an Elijah yet to come, whose ministry will be to restore:

> And His disciples asked Him, saying, "Why then do the scribes say that Elijah must come first?" Jesus answered and said to them, "Indeed, Elijah is coming first and will restore all things. But I say to you that Elijah has come already, and they did not know him but did to him whatever they wished.

Likewise the Son of Man is also about to suffer at their hands." Then the disciples understood that He spoke to them of John the Baptist (Matthew 17:10-13).

When we compare this passage with Acts 3:19-21, we make an amazing discovery. Scripture indicates that an "Elijah" is to rise before the Rapture. Just as the historic Elijah lived and prophesied to his day and then was raptured, so it will be with this promised Elijah:

> "Repent therefore and be converted, that your sins may be blotted out, so that times of refreshing may come from the presence of the Lord, and that He may send Jesus Christ, who was preached to you before, whom heaven must receive until the times of restoration of all things, which God has spoken by the mouth of all His holy prophets since the world began" (Acts 3:19-21).

Could the Elijah Jesus was speaking about be the last-days church? Can the church recover its voice from the spiritual laryngitis brought on by political and legalistic turmoil and herald the coming of Jesus Christ? The church today may very well be both the restorer and the restored preparing the way of the Lord! Look at Elijah!

1. *He appeared suddenly!* Scholars aren't sure of the roots and origins of the prophet Elijah, as he simply appeared out of history and blazed a path

of righteousness in his nation. In much the same way, the church was birthed when *suddenly* there came a sound from heaven at Pentecost, as a mighty rushing wind hit the disciples and filled them with Holy Spirit power. These men would spread abroad and turn nations upside down with the powerful message of Jesus!

2. *He came at a time of national and spiritual crisis.* Ahab and Jezebel, rulers in Elijah's day, had driven the nation into political chaos. The uncertainty, deceit, unrest and spiritual decay brought by their evil rule had wrought havoc with Israel. Likewise, our world has experienced a leadership vacuum and has been manipulated and deceived by many power-driven men.

3. *Elijah spoke for the Lord.* Acting as God's voice on earth, Elijah brought messages that his nation and its leaders had to hear, even some that were unpopular. Today the church holds that awesome responsibility.

4. *His prayer life was primary.* James 5:17, 18 recounts the powerful outcome of Elijah's prayers:

> Elijah was a man with a nature like ours, and he prayed earnestly that it would not rain; and it did not rain on the land for three years and six months. And he prayed again, and the heaven gave rain, and the earth produced its fruit.

Could it be that God is awaiting the cry of those of us in the church, desiring our passionate intercession for our nation and world? How deep is our burden for the souls of men and women? How far would you personally go in intercession and pleading for those who need God's saving power? How far into the world would you stretch your energies and resources to see souls come to Christ?

5. *He was gifted with supernatural power.* Miracles followed the ministry of Elijah. The hungry were fed, the needy were cared for, and the dead and dying were raised from death. The "last days" church should exhibit the same powerful supernatural signs, embracing the power of the Holy Spirit to heal and deliver those in need.

6. *Elijah lived by faith.* When living in the center of God's will, Elijah once found himself in a desert, without food or sustenance, but God sent ravens to feed him. He lived on God's provision alone. In this day when self-sufficiency is prized by the world, churches must return to believing that God is the sole source of our strength and power.

7. *Angels attended to his needs.* During his darkest times, angels came to Elijah to strengthen his heart and provide for his needs. Hebrews 1:14 indicates these same beings are available to us: "Are they not

all ministering spirits sent forth to minister for those who will inherit salvation?"

8. *He discovered his great need for others.* Elijah experienced a season of great loneliness. He thought he alone was left in faithful service to God! However, the Lord soon revealed to him that over 7,000 souls were on every side who had not yet bowed to the false god Baal. He was not alone! Today's church must get over the practice of denominational isolation and reach into the lives of believers everywhere to feed and support each other!

9. *Elijah came to restore the family.* His ministry and concern for the widow and her son represents Elijah's ever-present burden for the restoration of relationships in his nation. Malachi 4:5, 6 declared that the family must be changed and restored in the last days. Our world has seen the undermining of families through immorality, divorce, violence and declining values. The church should be a place where the family is lifted up and renewed.

10. *Elijah was not surprised by his rapture!* This great prophet was one of only two men in Scripture who was transported to heaven directly, without experiencing death! Elijah was taken to heaven in a whirlwind accompanied by chariots of fire.

Scripture tells us that the church will also be caught up one day as was Elijah:

> "For this we say to you by the word of the Lord, that we who are alive and remain until the coming of the Lord will by no means precede those who are asleep. For the Lord Himself will descend from heaven with a shout, with the voice of an archangel, and with the trumpet of God. And the dead in Christ will rise first. Then we who are alive and remain shall be caught up together with them in the clouds to meet the Lord in the air. And thus we shall always be with the Lord. Therefore comfort one another with these words" (1 Thessalonians 4:15-18).

There will likely be two groups of people in the church who will be surprised on the day of the Rapture. The first is those who are left behind, having never accepted Christ's gift of salvation, but choosing instead to futilely ride on their good works and good intentions to get them to heaven. The second group may be those who find themselves face-to-face with Christ in the air and suddenly realize that they never got around to the holiness and service for God they intended to do.

Our Ongoing Mission

All of these comparisons with Elijah brings Malachi into a new relevance for our day. His exposure of failed religion, wicked morals, financial unfaithfulness and other glaring problems speak to the church today. What is our call of duty in these last days?

- The church must be stirred to her prophetic calling! Even as Malachi's name meant "messenger," the church must lift up the message of the "Sun of Righteousness," who comes with healing in His wings.

- We must extend healing and forgiveness toward those who have experienced the pain of divorce and follow Scriptural principles for maintaining their ministry and fellowship in the body of Christ.

- We must also warn the lost that there is a burning, fiery hell awaiting them if they refuse the appeals of God's grace.

- Earnest appeals must be made to God's people, admonishing them to confess the sin of robbing God of tithes and offerings, and to begin generously sowing resources into the kingdom of God so that heaven can open over their lives.

- The church must pray with passion and pursue a love relationship with Jesus more than ever.

Let us look ahead with joy and gladness to the hope of the coming of Christ but not fail in our responsibility to this generation that desperately needs the overwhelming grace of God!